HEART & HOME

FOR CHRISTMAS

HEART & HOME

FOR CHRISTMAS

Celebrating Joy in Your Living Space

Victoria Duerstock

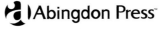
Abingdon Press™

NASHVILLE

HEART & HOME FOR CHRISTMAS
CELEBRATING JOY IN YOUR LIVING SPACE

Designed by Joy O'Meara

Library of Congress Cataloging-in-Publication Data

ISBN 978-1-5018-8543-3

19 20 21 22 23 24 25 26 27 28—10 9 8 7 6 5 4 3 2 1

MANUFACTURED IN THE PEOPLES REPUBLIC OF CHINA

The Christmas season comes roaring in faster and faster each year. It seems we barely survive the dog days of summer with its final last hurrah of Labor Day weekend, only to zip through the next few months like grabbing a tornado by the tail. Before we know it, we are starting a new year and counting down until summer again!

My heart's desire is for each of us to be able to grab just a few moments in these crazy days to ponder the depth of the meaning of Christmas to us personally. To view with awe the wonder of the miracle of Christ's birth, his life, and his death & resurrection and to celebrate the joy that truth brings to each of us.

I pray you will have a very Merry Christmas as you enjoy this season.

The use of an Advent calendar helps us count down with our children the days until Christmas morning. Whether you choose a method with a treat inside or a more simple version of counting down, building the excitement of Christmas morn is a lovely way to extend Christmas fun this season.

COUNTDOWN IS ON

"For the Lord Himself shall descend from heaven with a shout, with the voice of the archangel, and with the trump of God: and the dead in Christ shall rise first."

1 THESS. 4:16 (KJV)

*S*ometimes I wonder if Joseph ever asked Mary—is it time yet? Or maybe I should wonder *how many times* he asked in true first-time father fashion. What a countdown that must have been—not knowing what day or time—just simply being ready to answer the call to parent Jesus, the Savior of the World.

We count down many things in our lives too. Even now, we count down to Christmas to build the anticipation for our children with Advent calendars or activities to do each day leading up to the 25th.

It causes me to think of the countdown that we are still on today. As Christians, we look forward to having Christ return for His bride. We don't know the day or the hour, but we wait, and we watch for His return because He has proven himself faithful in the past to fulfill His promises. He will indeed come again and take us home to heaven. Knowing that this life is not the end brings me joy as I look expectantly for His return.

*Faithful Father, I look forward with great anticipation to
my home in heaven one day. Help me live my life in light of this great truth!*

SEASONAL DÉCOR TIP Nativity scenes come in a variety of styles—wood, bone china, papier-mâché—even ones specifically made for children's curious fingers! Using a Nativity scene in your Christmas décor is a great way to bring the proper focus to our celebrations. Let the simplicity of the manger remind all who see it of the Good News.

MEEK & MILD

"And she gave birth to her firstborn son and wrapped
Him in swaddling cloths and laid Him in a manger."

LUKE 2:7 (ESV)

*T*he King of Glory, a babe in a manger. God's only Son, Redeemer of all mankind. *Laid in a manger.* Indeed, God uses the humble things to confound the wise. Instead of a royal announcement, the shepherds heard from the angels. Instead of pomp and circumstance for the Lord of all creation and Messiah, Jesus had an unassuming birth to simple parents in a stall intended for animals.

A manger is simply a feeding trough for outdoor animals. Scripture tells us that work animals stay close to the manger because they can go there for sustenance. Now forgive me for comparing us to work animals like oxen, and bear with me a moment (the Bible does compare us to sheep, though!). If animals are conditioned to remain close to their source of food for the strength they need, how much more should we, as Christians, lean in and remain close to the message of the manger?

Lord, as I prepare my home for Christmas this year,
help my heart dwell on the truth of the simplicity
and humility of the manger.

SEASONAL TIP

The Christmas season sprinkles lots of grace around. I know we can't buy grace at a store, but I think that anytime we find ourselves anxious and stressed, we should stop to consider if our expectations are at fault. If so, we may need to be more flexible and filled with grace for whatever situation we are facing. Our families and our homes will be happier places if we put this in action.

HOW SHOULD A KING COME?

"Behold, the days are coming," declares the LORD,
"When I will raise up for David a righteous Branch; And He will reign as king."
JEREMIAH 23:5 (NASB)

*T*here's a lovely Christmas carol that talks about the expectation of the King's arrival for the Jews. The Savior, the King who was promised to the nation of Israel, didn't come as they expected. He came not as a King who conquered and vanquished all their human foes, but instead wrapped in our limited flesh as a helpless babe in a humble manger.

Do your expectations ever get shattered? Is reality a much different place than you expected it to be? The lesson here is that sometimes our expectations are just wrong. What expectations could you let go of today to make your heart a readier place for the Spirit of God to work in a mighty way and bring you joy?

Lord, I lay down every expectation
and faulty idea that is not from You. Show me
Your way, for I know it is higher
and better than my own.

MARY

And Mary said, "Behold, I am the servant of the Lord; let it be to me according to your word."

LUKE 1:38 (ESV)

The idea of submitting to anyone runs counter to our natures. The reality of taking my will, my dreams, and my desires and putting them under God's umbrella is very difficult sometimes. Most of the time, the reason for this is simple: my perspective is limited. I can only see what lies in front of me, not the big picture of all of Creation. Because I'm finite, my God—who is infinite and knows the beginning and the end—will have a different perspective than I do. The sooner I learn to submit to what His will is for me, the easier my road will be!

It reminds me of Mary—a young girl getting ready to embark and fulfill her marriage vow—and how she must have had her own plans in mind, but submitted to God's will to become the mother of Jesus, the Savior of the world! I can't imagine the weight of that submission, and the absolute fright it must have given her knowing Joseph's rights under Jewish law. But she trusted anyway, and she bowed her will to God's plan trusting His heart in the process.

Lord, help me to continue to learn to bow my will to Yours
and trust Your heart completely with whatever it is
I am having trouble releasing to You today.

SEASONAL DÉCOR TIP

One easy designer strategy in a decorating plan is to use symmetry. When you create balance in your vignettes and rooms in general, it is universally appealing. Balance creates calm and order. So whether you choose to have a lot of detail or keep your décor minimal, symmetry is always a winning choice.

—Jodie & Julie,
the Design Twins
www.thedesigntwins.com,
IG: @julie.thedesigntwins and
@jodie.thedesigntwinsabriel

JOSEPH

"You shall call His name Jesus, for He will save His people from their sins."
MATTHEW 1:21 (NASB)

*M*uch like I wonder what it must have been like for Mary as the mother of Jesus, I enjoy reflecting about Joseph, Jesus' earthly dad. It must have been difficult—raising Jesus to be a man, yet knowing He already had all and knew all He needed to. I can't even fathom this challenge, can you?

And yet Joseph taught Him what he knew including his trade of carpentry. Jesus was known not only as a carpenter, but as a carpenter's son. I can picture a young Jesus watching and learning from Joseph as they built and created new things.

Whether or not we have children, I believe it's important to pass on our skills to the next generation just as Joseph was faithful to do. While job skills are important, spiritual disciplines are even more so. The disciplines of Bible study, prayer, fasting, meditation, and memorization are important skills the next generation must learn. These skills are caught not taught. Being faithful to apply them in our own lives first gives us stronger impact and credibility when we seek to pass them on.

Make me an instrument of peace, dear Lord.
Help me to be faithful to train those in my care to follow
You through what has been taught to me.

SEASONAL DÉCOR TIP Having a dedicated place to read and pray is valuable. Create a spot in the bedroom with a chair and spruce it up this season to help create consistency in our walk. If your room is small, try grouping two to three smaller trees together in a corner. You can add ornaments, if desired, but lights and a tree skirt are often enough to create a warm and cozy Christmas bedroom.—Kathy Atkins www.livebeautifullyadorned.com, IG @beautifullyadorned

GABRIEL

"I am Gabriel, that stand in the presence of God; and am sent to speak unto thee, and to shew thee these glad tidings."

LUKE 1:19 (KJV)

Scripture records Gabriel's presence a handful of times. The book of Daniel speaks of Gabriel bringing Daniel the news that his prayers had been answered, but that spiritual warfare had delayed the message. Gabriel is also mentioned in the book of Luke as the angel delivering the Good News of babies to Zechariah, the father of John, and to Mary, the mother of Jesus.

He carried some of the greatest messages from heaven to earth and, with them, the understanding that everything was going exactly according to God's plan and not just happenstance.

Do you ever desire that clear word from God? A word of encouragement directly from heaven that will help you keep walking the walk? Sweet friend, we are so blessed to have that access to the Word. Each day, we can find comfort, direction, and encouragement for our daily lives. Making a consistent walk through the Bible is essential to our hearts and homes being exactly what it can—and should be—for Christ.

Father, keep me in Your Word daily so that I can continue to hear from You and lean on You for instruction on how to live this life.

STAR OF WONDER, STAR OF NIGHT

"A star shall come out of Jacob, and a scepter shall rise out of Israel."

NUMBERS 24:17 (ESV)

*P*rior to the birth of Christ, the prophecy of the Messiah's birth was taught not only to the Jews, but also to the people surrounding them. The Babylonian captivity was an event that brought great distress to the Jewish nation, but God redeemed this painful time by placing teachers of the Jewish tradition and the ancient manuscripts among Gentile and heathen nations so God could use them to also influence future generations and accomplish His purpose.

The night of Christ's birth, the sky was illuminated with a bright shining star—signaling to the world that the Christ child had been born. It was a signal for all those seeking Him. The star reminds us that He is available to be found by those who seek Him. I am reminded that sometimes the most difficult moments in our lives are opportunities for God to step in and grow our faith. God receives the greatest glory in our lives, and it's more evident when God turns our difficulties into blessings. While the Jewish captivity was not planned or wanted, God used the situation for good by allowing the next generations to seek Him.

Lord, thank You for allowing those who seek You to find You and for redeeming our darkest hours to bring You glory.

SEASONAL DÉCOR TIP Wrap presents in kraft paper. This works with any décor style, because you can add your own style with washi tape designs, ribbons, and ornaments or even artistic drawings and designs on the outside of the package. Create something special and unique with your wrapping!

STARRY NIGHTS

"When they saw the star, they rejoiced with exceeding great joy."
MATTHEW 2:10 (KJV)

I haven't always been a star watcher, but I must admit to having a certain affinity with the night sky these days. You see, several years ago I decided that I was going to make my quiet time with the Lord a priority. This meant sacrificing some sleep and getting up at 5 o'clock in the morning—most days before the dawn! The amazing side benefit (besides the consistent time to spend with God, the blissful peace and quiet, and coffee—can I hear an Amen?) was the opportunity to learn about the sky. Using a night sky app on my phone, I could see which planets were rising, where the stars were, and even the occasional space station. Watching the sun rise each morning after the planets and stars disappeared became a favorite ritual and one that makes this passage special to me.

You see, the wise men had been taught the passage from the book of Numbers about the star rising from Jacob. They knew the star was important because they also studied the night sky and knew when something special had appeared on the horizon—without any fancy app on their phones! What a delight to see the promise of God in the stars. He is faithful, my friends—His Word is always true.

*Thank You, Lord, for the beauty of Your creation
and Your faithfulness toward me, Lord!*

SEASONAL DÉCOR TIP While the work of decorating and preparing our homes for Christmas can be overwhelming, there are things that can be done to save time. Keeping all your decorations in one location or corner and clearly labeled can make the decorating process much easier the next year. Don't let the rush of putting all the things away push you to neglect clearly marking and storing those items. Your future self will thank you!

SHEPHERDS

"And in the same region there were shepherds out in the field, keeping watch over their flock by night."
LUKE 2:8 (ESV)

The Good News of the Savior's birth was brought not to the cultural elite—not to the kings and queens and temple leaders. Rather the Good News was heralded from the angels to the shepherds while they were working. When the angel of the Lord appeared to bring them the Good News, they were filled with fear. The heavenly host of angels told them not to fear and shared what wondrous thing had occurred that night. After they heard the Good News they turned and went to Bethlehem to seek Him Who had been heralded.

Many times in our spiritual journey we will receive answers to the hard questions we have been asking in the middle of our work. While we are carrying the tasks of our everyday lives, sometimes God shows up and makes our next steps VERY obvious.

Lord, I thank You that You meet us all in the places where our need is greatest. While we live our lives, You show up and give us just what we need to accomplish Your will.

SEASONAL DÉCOR

TIP Mixing new and vintage pieces is an easy way to add drama to a table setting. Adding vintage items such as milk glass or cut-glass crystal to inexpensive newer items such as unbreakable chargers and simple white glass plates adds a richness and authenticity that won't break your budget. Also don't be afraid to mix different styles with your vintage pieces. Four different milk glass goblets can be even more interesting than a matching set.

—Brandy Bell,
www.sobellandco.com,
IG @sobellandco

ANSWERED PRAYER

"Do not be afraid, Zechariah, for your prayer has been heard,
and your wife Elizabeth will bear you a son, and you shall call his name John."

LUKE 1:13 (ESV)

The story of this couple is one that many are familiar with. Infertility is a tough journey for anyone to travel. For those who love the Lord and find their desires unmet in this area, the pain feels visceral. Many important men of Scripture were born to mothers who had been childless—including John the Baptist. The births of these men to these mothers were made even more precious by the longing and waiting for their sons. Struggling with infertility can be a painful and sorrowful time in a couple's marriage.

But Zechariah experienced both joy and doubt when he was told of his special blessing. Isn't it something, my friend, that when we receive an answer to a long-awaited request, we can't even believe it? We pray with such little faith that we are surprised when God moves the mountains in our way.

Is there something you are petitioning God for even today? Remember the lesson of Elizabeth and Zechariah and pray believing—no matter how long it takes!

God, I thank You for the reality of answered prayers
and Your goodness to each of us. You are so good.

SEASONAL TIP As you talk through the Christmas story with your family and friends, explore how the story might have been different if there had been room in the inn for Him after all. Consider ways to share the many blessings you and your family share. Find areas to serve a meal, help a family purchase gifts, or donate your time to help a friend or family in need.

NO ROOM IN THE INN

"And she gave birth to her firstborn son and wrapped him in swaddling cloths and laid him in a manger, because there was no place for them in the inn."

LUKE 2:7 (ESV)

*D*o you ever hold back a part of yourself or your home because there is no more room? Overwhelmed with busyness no matter the season, I tend to shut down my availability when I'm stressed. And truth be told, I do need to protect my time and space at times, but I can also turn away the needs of others around me when I'm too far unbalanced with my desire for space.

Do you ever think how the story of Christ's birth might have unfolded if there had been room in the inn? Would the wonder of the lowliness of His birth have gotten lost if His arrival hadn't been so unusual? I believe that He came in humility and simplicity to extend His grace to each and every one of us. This is a connection we can all receive no matter our station or lot in life. The King of the World and Jesus the Friend of Sinners are one and the same. No matter where we fall on the poverty line, He came for us all.

I praise You, God, for being the Savior of all mankind.
You are truly our great Redeemer.

SEASONAL DÉCOR TIP Decorating our homes with gold ornaments and accents helps create a warm and luxurious feeling. Accents of silver and glitter paper chains on eucalyptus garland can dress up a banister or mantel quickly and easily.

GOLD, FRANKINCENSE & MYRRH

"And going into the house, they saw the child with Mary His mother, and they fell down and worshiped Him. Then, opening their treasures, they offered Him gifts, gold and frankincense and myrrh."

MATTHEW 2:11 (ESV)

*T*he precious and valuable treasures brought from distant lands by the wise men remind us who the Christ child really was. The seekers from the Orient spent great time and energy—not to mention resources—to find these gifts. At their first meeting with King Herod, they told him that this babe was born the King of the Jews.

How did these wise men know that Jesus' birth was remarkable and wonderful? While it's possible that the Jewish nation influenced these wise men before the Captivity, it's more likely that this generation of wise men was influenced by the Jews who arrived during the Babylonian Captivity. Although facing consequences for their sinful behaviors and now living far from home, the children of Israel still worshipped, prayed, and lived out their faith among strangers, much as many of us live out our lives today. Because of this faithful witness, the teachings were passed from generation to generation. The wise men made a long journey over four hundred years later to see with their eyes what they believed in faith. May we all have a faithful witness that will be shared in this same way!

Lord, I pray that You'll remind me to be faithful to proclaim the Good News to those You surround me with even today.

SEASONAL DÉCOR TIP If you are a DIYer you likely have leftover scraps from various projects. Mosaics have always fascinated me because small pieces are used to create a larger overall picture of beauty. Broken china can be repurposed. Even leftover tile can be used to make tree ornaments or gift toppers with an added touch of ribbon or foil lettering.

BROKEN BETHLEHEM

"But thou, Bethlehem Ephrathah, though thou be little among the thousands of Judah, yet out of thee shall he come forth unto Me that is to be ruler in Israel; whose goings forth have been from of old, from everlasting."

MICAH 5:2 (KJV)

*G*od chooses the weak things to use for His glory. Have you noticed evidence of this in your own life? I have. He tends to use my weaknesses to display His strength and power. I know it's so He will receive all the glory from the experience I am going through, but sometimes it would be nice if He worked from my strengths! Ha.

A recent Bible study of the Old Testament reminded me of God using the weak for glory in the humble town of Bethlehem. The history may not seem so nice, but a redemptive story rose from the ashes because of Christ's birth. Not only did Jesus fulfill the prophecy in Micah, but He also used a town of people who hadn't always done the right thing.

Isn't that just music to your ears, though? God can still use us, broken, bloodied, full of fault, and less than innocent. He will accomplish His great work in us because He has promised to finish what He has started in us.

Lord, I praise You for Your patience to complete Your work in us.
Thank You for using us, weak and broken though we are.

SEASONAL DÉCOR TIP Using a manger as a focal point for Christmas décor is a lovely way to call us to worship and remember God's signs to the shepherds. A small manger can be placed by the tree, on a table, or near the front door. The visual reminder of the sign helps right our focus during this busy season.

WATCH THE SIGNS

"This will be a sign to you: You will find a baby wrapped in cloths and lying in a manger."

LUKE 2:12 (NIV)

*I*n our daily lives, we use signs to navigate where we drive, in decorating our homes, and to help us make decisions. Like Gideon with the fleece, we want to see a clear sign in the sky or writing on the wall to give us the answers we seek. Sometimes, we have to make the next right move and walk in faith that He will continue to guide our next step. The birth of Christ was heralded to the shepherds with a sign. The manger itself—the humblest of beds and birthplaces—was the sign that indeed they had found not just a baby, but THE baby—the Savior of man, the Messiah!

During the Christmas season, we are reminded to adore the precious Christ child. The call rings loud and clear to come and adore Him, Christ the Lord. A sign to leave behind all other things and simply worship Him.

I long to abandon all other tasks, necessary or pleasurable,
to be present with You, Lord. Help me be aware of the signs
you are sending me and follow you in obedience.

THE HEAVENLY HOST,
THE ONES WHO PRAISED

"And suddenly there was with the angel a multitude of the heavenly host praising God, and saying,
Glory to God in the highest, and on earth peace, good will toward men."

LUKE 2:13-14 (KJV)

As soon as the message from the first angel was delivered to the shepherds, a heavenly host of angels joined the single angel and gloriously praised God in the midst of the night sky. Can you just imagine it? First one angel telling you not to fear, and then a host of angels raising their voices in praise right in front of you! It must have been a spectacular sight to behold.

See, my friend, God doesn't need us to praise Him and bring Him glory, but He wants us to. The Bible teaches that even the rocks would cry out in praise if there is silence, but He longs to hear our voices lifted in worship.

We can praise Him when we are praying or when we are singing.
We can praise Him when we are vacuuming or dusting.
We can praise Him when are happy or sad.
We can praise Him on the mountain or in the valley.
There's so much to praise Him for!

Lord, I praise You for who You are! I thank You that my praise is a sweet-smelling
offering to You. May it always be on my lips.

SEASONAL DÉCOR TIP Don't be afraid to mix real and faux greenery. I often incorporate real and faux greenery into tablescapes, garlands, and wreaths. You can make inexpensive wreaths and garlands look and smell full and beautiful by simply layering in real pine branches into the faux wired pieces.

—Brandy Bell www.sobellandco.com

IG- @sobellandco

ELIZABETH, THE ONE WHO REJOICED

"And when Elizabeth heard the greeting of Mary, the baby leaped in her womb. And Elizabeth was filled with the Holy Spirit, and she exclaimed with a loud cry, 'Blessed are you among women, and blessed is the fruit of your womb!'"

LUKE 1:41-42 (ESV)

*I*magine the scene here and if you have time to read further, go read the entire passage in Luke. It's truly special. The angel not only shared that Mary would carry Jesus, but also that Elizabeth was carrying a son after many long years of waiting. Mary rushed to Elizabeth's home in excitement—can you imagine the giddy gathering? We girls can squeal with excitement, but what stands out to me is that baby John in Elizabeth's womb leaped for joy at the sound of Mary's voice. What a special moment indeed! Elizabeth was filled with the spirit and blessed Mary too. Her son John was the forerunner for Christ. He was sent to prepare the world's hearts and minds for Christ. We can see how the Holy Spirit was at work in advance of Jesus' birth preparing His way.

I'm so thankful there was a redemption plan. Without it, I'd still be lost in my sin with no way of reconciling with God. But then came Jesus. What Good News!

Thank You, Lord, for the sweet record in Scripture of the excitement of two expecting women. Thank You for recording such a sweet scene for us to know.

SEASONAL TIP During this season consider keeping a journal. Detail prayer requests and answers you receive. Pull the journal out each year and review how God has answered prayers and been faithful in your life. Each year add to it and provide a legacy for your family to read through even when you are gone.

SIMEON, THE ONE WHO WAITED

"And, behold, there was a man in Jerusalem, whose name was Simeon . . . waiting for the consolation of Israel."

LUKE 2:25 (KJV)

One of my favorite stories of the Christmas season has to do with Simeon meeting the baby Jesus in the temple. Described as righteous and devout, Simeon longed for the Messiah. Further reading tells us that the Holy Spirit was upon him. God even promised him that he would see Christ before he died. When Mary and Joseph brought Jesus to the temple to be presented to the Lord, Simeon felt compelled to also come to the temple. He took the babe in his arms and knew exactly who He was—Jesus Christ—and he praised God. What a beautiful picture of a promise received!

How about you, friend? Have you been waiting for God to fulfill promises in your life? Maybe you are praying for the salvation of a family member or friend. Maybe you are praying for faith to trust in God's promise of provision for a certain need, but His timing doesn't match up with yours. No matter the case, you can trust that God's promises always come true. He is faithful and true and worthy of our every admiration.

Father, I thank You for the promises You've fulfilled in the past,
and the promises I know You are faithful to fulfill in the future.

SEASONAL TIP Christmas is the easiest time to invite others in. Inviting new and old friends into our homes allows us the opportunity to share the Good News of the gospel with family, friends, and neighbors alike. Many who normally might feel uncomfortable in this situation may feel more open to the message of Jesus. He is the reason for the season.

ANNA, THE ONE WHO WITNESSED

"And there was one Anna . . . And she coming in that instant gave thanks likewise unto the Lord, and spake of Him to all them that looked for redemption in Jerusalem."

LUKE 2:36-38 (KJV)

Anna enters a joyous scene of celebration during the dedication of the Christ child. In the temple, Mary and Joseph, encouraged by Simeon, encounter Anna as well. Anna devoted her life to God and service in the temple. Because she was so in tune with Him, she knew immediately that she had just met the Son of God. The Messiah had come!

Being devoted to God includes service in our worship. Fasting, Bible study, and prayer should be constants. Not growing tired or bored in this work, but actually increasing your time and enjoying worshipping our Father, even as Anna continued to serve year after year. From there, we will be overflowing with the Good News for others. We should be willing, able, and eager to share what Christ's birth means for us as it pointed to His death and resurrection and our ultimate rescue.

Father, I thank You for the gift of the Savior
and pray that I will be faithful to share the Good News to all who will hear.

SEASONAL TIP When decorating a room such as a bedroom, it doesn't take much to change the entire room. Adding garland above the headboard and tucking a tree beside the bed is sometimes all that is needed. Kathy Atkins livebeautifullyadorned.com, IG @beautifullyadorned

MARY'S MAGNIFICAT

"And Mary said, 'My soul magnifies the Lord, and my spirit rejoices in God my Savior.'"
LUKE 1:46-47 (ESV)

Scripture does not record many details of Mary dealing with the big life change of becoming a new mother, let alone being newly pregnant with the promised Messiah. We read only how Gabriel shared the news with her that she'd been chosen, and we hear her acceptance. We do learn that after Elizabeth hears her blessing, Mary sings a song of praise to the Lord, which is often referred to as Mary's Magnificat. At the very least, we can assume that Mary must have had parents who loved the Word of God and faithfully taught it to her. The song recorded here in Luke was filled with biblical truths she must have been taught. Even the style of the song was reminiscent of Old Testament poetry and music.

Magnificat means to magnify or enlarge. Mary's song was about bringing glory to God, where it rightfully belonged. While she knew all eyes would be on her with many not understanding her and assuming untruths, Mary knew deep in her heart what an honor God had blessed her with.

Many of us will not face a spotlight quite like the one Mary had, but anytime someone wants to know what we are doing and why, I pray we will be ready with an answer that brings glory and magnifies the Lord at work in us.

*I praise You, Lord, and magnify Your name because You are good,
and Your mercy endures forever!*

SEASONAL DÉCOR TIP Consider using a white fluffy shag rug or faux fur rug in front of your Christmas tree. Not only is it cozy for sitting on, on Christmas morning, but it also gives the aesthetic of snowy white ground cover!

Oh, the weather outside is frightful but the fire is so delightful and since we've no place to go Let it snow. Let it snow. Let it snow

STILL, WE WAIT

"But for You, O LORD, do I wait; it is You, O Lord my God, Who will answer."
PSALM 38:15 (ESV)

*S*cripture tells us the Messiah—the promised Redeemer of all—was prophesized many years before Jesus was born. The Jews had waited so long for this—for God incarnate come to earth as the Christ child, fully God and fully man.

Jesus came and redeemed us—past, present, and future sins all forgiven in one cataclysmic event that shook the world to its very core. And yet still we wait. We wait now for the next promise of His glorious return to carry His bride home to heaven.

Do you ever feel like the waiting takes forever? Do you remember as a child, how it seemed to take so long for Christmas morning to arrive? Or Christmas mornings with little ones who can't seem to wait to open their next gift? They open so quickly that without intervention they don't actually get to enjoy the gift they opened because they want what's next.

How often do we react the same way? Anxious to move forward to the next thing, we grow weary waiting for God to do something. But time is of no matter to God—He is timeless, but we are impatient. Yet God always fulfills His promises.

Thank You, God, for being faithful to fulfill Your promises.
I praise You for Your faithfulness.

SEASONAL DÉCOR TIP

Let your home be warm and welcoming and inviting. Let it say, "Come! Spend time here and feel comfortable." Don't be so focused on decorating that guests are afraid to sit and relax. One of my favorite decorations are pillows because you can just throw them on the ground to make room to sit. Or we just sit on them!

—Jenny Scholten
IG @scholten_family_ceo

SILENT NIGHT STILLNESS

"Be still, and know that I am God."
PSALM 46:10 (KJV)

*N*ighttime quiet and predawn darkness are my quiet solace. It's in the quiet that I can still my restless mind and focus. These days, I mostly rise early to enjoy a quiet house, hot coffee, time to read my Bible, and prayer. This focused time of concentration allows me to dig deeper and really listen. Whether the night of Christ's birth was silent or not, we can appreciate the reminder to be still and listen!

What about you? Do you experience stillness from time to time? Do you embrace it or run? Do you need to be always busy? I have to admit that I crave the stillness and calm. This doesn't mean I'm not tired when I wake up early, but I find that it's easier to get moving when I know the precious sacredness that awaits me. Let's be honest, sometimes I still struggle to push myself to get out of the bed, but the effort is valuable. Making this early quiet time a priority and doing it consistently gives me a strong foundation to facing my day.

Lord, I thank You for the quiet I find in the night.
Thank You for drawing my attention and centering my thoughts in this season on You.

SEASONAL TIP I make it a point to get up early Christmas Eve morning, while everyone else is sleeping, just to sit quietly by the fire with a hot cup of tea and meditate on the meaning of the season. It helps me stay focused and not get too consumed in the hustle and bustle of the coming days.—Pamela Saumure IG @pamela.saumure

MARY, DID YOU KNOW?

"And Mary said, 'Behold the handmaid of the Lord; be it unto me according to thy word.'"
LUKE 1:38 (KJV)

As the mother of a perfect child, I wonder if it was encouraging and easy or overwhelmingly mind-boggling for Mary to be His mom. Raising and disciplining this child looked very different for Joseph and Mary than it does for you and me!

In addition, she knew His life would end in misery, suffering, and pain. Understanding that His purpose was to die a sacrificial death would be utterly heartbreaking, but the agony of these details was not revealed to her in foreknowledge. There's such a difference in knowing and KNOWING.

I wonder how many of us would be willing to take on that kind of task. This Christmas, I pray you'll appreciate the story of Mary. Think about your own response to what He might be calling you to do. I don't think any of us will have to make quite as large a sacrifice as Mary did.

*I thank You, Father, for making Mary an integral part
of the Christmas story. Help me to be a willing vessel for
Your service when You call on me to do an impossible task.*

SEASONAL DÉCOR TIP
A fun way to combine items you likely already have is to take picture frames with glass removed and combine ornaments with a plush ribbon and hang in a gallery fashion on a wall. Vary the lengths of ribbon and use a variety of greenery, ornaments, and frame styles.

EVERLASTING FATHER

"For to us a child is born, to us a son is given; and the government shall be upon his shoulder, and his name shall be called Wonderful Counselor, Mighty God, Everlasting Father."

ISAIAH 9:6 (ESV)

I love to study the different names of God. There is such comfort in knowing and understanding who God is, and the names we call Him give us clear indication of His nature. As we explore more about this child—the promised Savior and Messiah—the title of Everlasting Father is such a personal connection. There is something so precious and tender about the love between a parent and child that allows us to understand the love that God promised to us. The designation of Everlasting Father reminds me of the personal access I have to Abba, and the fact that He always has been and always will be.

Not all earthly Fathers or parents are compassionate and loving, and that's truly unfortunate because we only have this earthly comparison to relate to Jesus as Father. But the perfect Everlasting Father is the One who will carry us through whatever we experience no matter the circumstances.

Lord, thank You for being from everlasting to everlasting—
always the same and unchanging. You father us with perfect love.

Gift wrap matches the tree décor. I wrap the gifts, and our daughters add ribbons and embellishments to each package.

—Pamela Saumure,
IG @pamela.saumure

WONDERFUL COUNSELOR

"For to us a child is born, to us a son is given; and the government shall be upon his shoulder,
and His name shall be called Wonderful Counselor."

ISAIAH 9:6 (ESV)

So many times we find ourselves in difficult predicaments. Maybe through no fault of our own, circumstances can be difficult. Job loss, death of a loved one, financial difficulty—they are all part of the ongoing battles we face in this life. Sometimes we just need to vent, and we look to our earthly friendships to fill our desire for consolation and comfort. But the perfect, most wonderful and faithful Counselor is already available and ready at any time—day or night. He provides our every need, including the emotional needs of love, care, and wise counsel. He ministers to our spirits, comforts, and provides.

This season, while many celebrate, some wear masks hiding their difficulties. Don't be someone who hides behind a mask—celebrate the joy of our Wonderful Counselor. Those we see wearing masks need help seeing the truth of the Wonderful Counselor so they may know the deep joy of knowing Christ.

You are a Wonderful Counselor and friend.
Thank You, Lord, for the gift of access to Your wise counsel and encouragement.

SEASONAL DÉCOR

TIP Chunky knit blankets are found in homes and showrooms everywhere right now. One new way to use the chunky blanket is wrapped around the base of a Christmas tree. It provides amazing texture and feel compared to a more traditional tree skirt.

THE MIGHTY GOD

"For to us a child is born, to us a Son is given; and the government shall be upon His shoulder, and His name shall be called Wonderful Counselor, Mighty God."

ISAIAH 9:6B (ESV)

*T*he promise of the babe in a manger included the promise of Him being the mighty God. The character of God that makes Him mighty includes not only being all powerful but also being mighty to save. Our redemption from this fallen sinful world is the beautiful reason for the season. The baby Jesus was just a part of the story—don't miss the bigger perspective! The mighty God Himself, as Jesus incarnate, was wrapped as a babe in that manger. While He could have been born in a palace or come to earth as the mighty conquering King He is, He came in the veil of our limited humanity to be at home among us. Only One Who is this mighty could choose to limit His strength in such a way. Only One this mighty could save all of the world.

There's nothing in my life that God's might cannot conquer. While we are in this world and will have trouble, we know that He has overcome the world. His might will rule one day again and will right all wrongs.

I praise You, mighty God, for being strong enough to defeat death and the grave. You alone are mighty to save.

SEASONAL TIP Keeping it simple promotes peace in our homes. Whether gifting our families with an adventure versus gifts, or limiting gifts to just a few categories, simplicity provides the canvas to rest in.

THE PRINCE OF PEACE

"His name shall be called Wonderful Counselor, Mighty God, Everlasting Father, Prince of Peace."
ISAIAH 9:6 (ESV)

*W*orld peace. Everyone longs for it and it's the favorite answer of beauty contestants when asked how they would change the world. During the Christmas season we sing songs of peace, but how do we actually achieve it? It can feel impossible at times to have our hearts at peace—let alone our households and even more difficult in our churches and communities. Sin has wreaked havoc on this land and in us. We long for peace, but we forget the source of peace is found in God alone. You can't find it in government or law, not religion or oath, but only in the One Who came as the Prince of Peace. His death on the cross brought us peace according to Ephesians 2 " *But now in Christ Jesus ye who sometimes were far off are made nigh by the blood of Christ. For He is our peace, Who hath made both one, and hath broken down the middle wall of partition between us."*

Indeed, peace will come from no other place than heaven itself. While the devil has his way on this earth, we know his end is coming. While we struggle with the effects of sin and destruction, we can rest assured that Christ will bring His peace into our lives.

Lord, I thank You during this stressful season that you are our Prince of peace. In a world of uncertainty, I run to You to keep my heart at rest.

SEASONAL DÉCOR TIP

Sometimes we don't have room to decorate a personalized tree for all the members of the household. A wreath can be a fun way to give some creative freedom to other members of your house as well! And honestly the themes are endless—toys, candy, and more can be used to enhance your wreath.

ADVENT

"The people who walked in darkness have seen a great light,
those who dwelt in a land of deep darkness, on them has light shone."

ISAIAH 9:2 (ESV)

The original Advent wreath began as a wagon wheel with red and white candles and has progressed into a more traditional-style wreath with the Advent candles nestled in. Many churches and families celebrate Advent during the four Sundays before Christmas with special services around each Advent word with some variations. Here's an example:

Week 1—Hope: The prophets waited in hope for the Messiah.

Week 2—Faith: The prophecy in Micah foretold that the Messiah would be born in Bethlehem.

Week 3—Joy: The shepherds rejoiced when the angels announced that Jesus came for all men.

Week 4—Peace: The Angels announced that Jesus came to bring peace.

Many times a fifth candle is lit on Christmas Eve. This is a lovely way to prepare our hearts and minds for the beauty of His birth. Using wreaths in our décor is an easy way to add a touch of greenery by bringing the outdoors inside. Beginning with the same basic foundation, each wreath can be personalized with colors and decorations that tell a unique story.

Lord, I thank You for the organized reminder an Advent study can bring to our hearts this season.
May we be conscientious of the hope, faith, joy, and peace that You came to bring to us all.

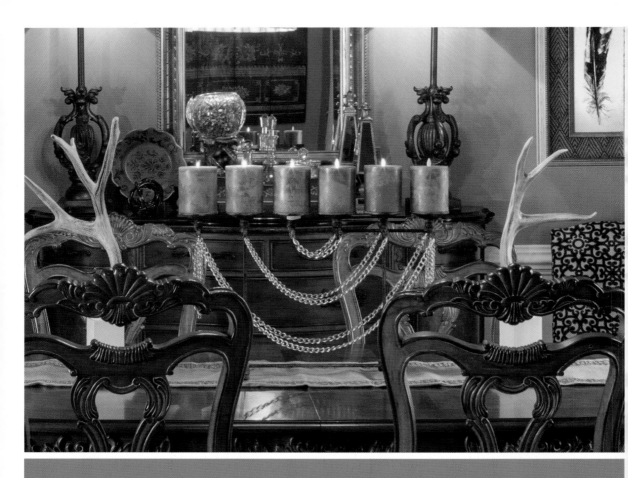

SEASONAL DÉCOR TIP Candles are such an integral part of decorating. From the traditional taper, or block to tealights, and even dripless or LED candles. They add such a pleasant ambiance to a room with their warm glow when lit. Purchase candles throughout the year in standard and neutral colors to mix in with the traditional Christmas scene.

PRAYER OF BLESSING

"The LORD bless you and keep you; the LORD make His face shine upon you and be gracious to you; the LORD turn His face toward you and give you peace."

NUMBERS 6:24-26 (NIV)

*O*ne of the greatest encouragements for me is when people pray for me. Having people support a project or a specific request by lifting me up in prayer helps me to push through a difficult season. But there's nothing like that personal touch with an in-person meeting when someone prays out loud—especially for me. It makes such an emotional connection and energizes me in a way that I can't explain. I know it means something special to God as well since He records for us in His Word the words given to Aaron to pray over the people.

During this time of gathering, I'd love to encourage you to be specific in your prayers for your family and friends. Let their presence remind you to pray, and if it's appropriate, stop what you are doing and pray out loud in person. Praying together in unity can bond people together like nothing else. Give your family the gift of being prayed over and continue throughout the year keeping them before the Lord.

Father, help me to remember what a difference it makes when people pray for me so that I will be faithful to pray for them.

SEASONAL DÉCOR TIP Look for ways to include your children in decorating. This is especially true for Christmas. It's the perfect way to teach them the beauty that can be found not only in the décor but also in spending time with one another creating memories.

—Kelly Radcliff IG @thetatteredpew

THE DELIGHT OF THE CHILDREN

"Let the little children come to Me and do not hinder them, for to such belongs the kingdom of heaven."
MATTHEW 19:14 (ESV)

The excitement of children during the Christmas season is delightful. From the time children are old enough to understand, they enjoy the festivities and traditions of Christmas, and decorating is one of those times! Create a sense of fun while decorating by including them in the process. You could give them their very own tree to decorate as a kid's Christmas tree that contains their favorite ornaments. Or you could decorate the family tree together with all the ornaments you've collected throughout the years, explaining to your child their personal meaning and including them in such a special time.

It reminds me of how much Jesus loved children. In a society and time when women and children were not always seen with value, Jesus welcomed them and loved children wholeheartedly. He included them when He was on this earth and instructed others not to stop them from excitedly coming to Him. I can't help but wonder if He longs for us to respond to Him in a childlike way. Excitement, joy, and enthusiasm all overflow in His presence. If this isn't your stance before Him, maybe you should reconsider your approach to Him.

I thank You, Lord, that You made room for the children.
I praise You for the joy You overflow into my life.

SEASONAL TIP As you become busier this season with the hustle and bustle of activity, don't forget to take the time as you decorate to talk with your children and share the importance of the celebration in this season. Share with them the Gospel and why it's such Good News!

CELEBRATE THE SEASON TOGETHER

"The Word became flesh and made His dwelling among us. We have seen His glory, the glory of the One and only Son, Who came from the Father, full of grace and truth."

JOHN 1:14 (NIV)

*I*f you are anything like me, you are amazed at the speed by which years fly by! Before you know it, the Christmas music is playing again, and the planning is wide open for all the decorating. Purists will complain that we shouldn't be listening to Christmas music, watching Christmas movies, or having Christmas parties until after the Thanksgiving holiday has passed, but in all honesty, if I wait that long to decorate, I might as well not do it! There just isn't enough time.

Christmas decorating trends vary from year to year. But you can always count on a solid traditional décor with red and green, plaids and velvets, and Nativity scenes. Contemporary décor highlights the whimsy with fun color palettes, Santa, Frosty, and more.

No matter your style, the greatest gift of the season is the promise kept with Jesus' birth, and the celebration continues today—so many lifetimes later. When we take the time to decorate our homes with the latest art, pillows, and ornaments, it allows conversations from day to day why we as Christians treasure the joy of this season.

Lord thank you for being my exceeding joy.
May this joy overflow into my home filling it with peace and comfort.

SEASONAL TIP We have a yearly tradition in our home for Christmas Eve. We always open one gift, but we pick it out for the kids. Each year we also buy them new Christmas pajamas and then we watch a movie, drink hot chocolate, and then head to bed (or to wrap more presents for the morning)!

ANTICIPATION

"Now faith is the assurance of things hoped for, the conviction of things not seen."

HEBREWS 11:1 (ESV)

Christmas Eve is a fun evening. The little ones always fight going to sleep. Children sneaking out of bed for a peek at the tree and presents is pretty common. You can almost feel the breathless anticipation of Christmas morning. I imagine the heavens must have waited in anticipation for Christ's birth as well. Hope birthed into our world that night and the promise fulfilled in a moment's time.

Faith in our lives should have the same sense of anticipation. We rest in faith because we are assured of the outcome. In light of this, we should be on the edge of our seats, anticipating how God is going to move on our behalf. Yet, many times I'm afraid that we live our lives in worry and fear that—while we wish to have faith, we are afraid of disappointment. Friends, do you have something you are waiting in faith for God to do for you? Are you waiting in anticipation and excitement or are you worried and anxious?

Father, help me live out faith in my life
just as young children anticipate Christmas morning.

TIP To create a festive holiday home use the simple technique of repetition. Repetition creates a uniform look. It also makes a statement. I created my festive holiday kitchen with mini faux wreaths and one large spool of ribbon. I used hot glue to attach the ribbon to each wreath. Then I attached the ribbon to the top backs of the cabinets using Velcro adhesive Command Strips.

—Jodie & Julie,
the Design Twins
www.thedesigntwins.com,
IG: @julie.thedesigntwins
and @jodie.thedesigntwins

OPEN DOORS & HEARTS

"They broke bread in their homes and ate together with glad and sincere hearts."
ACTS 2:46 (NIV)

*T*he early church provides an excellent example on opening our homes to others during this season. Scripture shows us that the disciples made time to be together frequently, enjoying meals together, and forging bonds of friendship based on deep roots of truths of God's Word.

While our society doesn't operate the same way anymore, we can still look to their example for developing relationships even today. This season is the easiest to be open and hospitable. Most of us have our homes decorated nicely for family coming to town—there's usually plates of cookies, hot chocolate, and something yummy cooking on the stove. While the schedule might be full of activities, there are others around us who might not have activities or family to be with. While I don't have all the answers, I know that I long for that openness with others.

Don't be afraid to invite others over. And don't tell me your place is a mess! Invite them over anyway. Let's just be real with people and stop trying to pretend we have it all together.

Lord, help me see those around me in need of a warm touch or kind word.
May I have a heart and home open for those You love.

SEASONAL DÉCOR TIP Grab any extra baskets or a storage ottoman or decorative box to keep near your entrance. This gives folks a place to lay their things without putting them in your way. You can also straighten up a spare bedroom as a place for guests to lay their coats, purses, etc.

LESS IS MORE

"Take My yoke upon you, and learn from Me, for I am gentle and lowly in heart, and you will find rest for your souls. For My yoke is easy, and My burden is light."

MATTHEW 11:29-30 (ESV)

Sometimes less is more in an entrance area—whether it's your back door or front door. It's great to designate an area for people to hang their coats or purses. Baskets for gloves or shoes or an area for odds and ends can make the experience easier for guests entering your home. Unencumbered of their extra stuff, people can relax and enjoy themselves in your home.

Similarly, this is just as it should be as I enter my time with the Lord each morning or evening. I imagine laying down all of my extra gear and baggage before I come in to sit at His feet. Perhaps it's even more impactful to envision at the end of a long day—leaving all your burdens behind to sit and dwell with the One Who sees and knows all that we carry. Whether you meet Him in the still of the morning or at the end of the day—find Him there and dwell. Here we find rest.

I praise You, oh God, for being a God Who bears my burdens.
Help me leave those things behind and dwell with You without distraction.

SEASONAL TIP There's a plethora of choices when it comes to choosing holiday scent: candles, wax melters, air fresheners, diffusers, and more. Whether essential oils or regular fragrance, keep in mind that some struggle with headaches and other allergic reactions triggered by scents. Keep the smells coming, just don't overdo it! If you know you have guests coming, be sensitive not to overwhelm your guests.

THE SMELLS OF CHRISTMAS

"And walk in love, as Christ loved us and gave Himself up for us, a fragrant offering and sacrifice to God."
EPHESIANS 5:2 (ESV)

Christmas is a season overflowing with amazing smells. Whether you like the baking scents of vanilla, cinnamon, or snickerdoodle, or you prefer the outdoor scents of the pine, sap, or greenery—the smell of Christmas is unmistakable. Christmas food smells are abundant because so many of us find ourselves in the kitchen making food for family, gifts for friends, and cookies for our kids' school parties. Peppermints, hot chocolate, or apple cider fill the air, and our mind reminisces of sweet Christmases of times gone by.

Smells are mentioned in the Bible too. There are several passages where the people offered a sacrifice to the Lord and it was a sweet smell to Him. Ephesians 5:2 reminds us that the sacrificial Lamb—Jesus—was the ultimate sweet-smelling fragrant offering. When we walk in love together, we offer the same sacrifice of self to a Holy God who enjoys its sweet smell.

Lord, I pray that I will walk in love, sacrificing my selfish desires for others and in turn becoming a fragrant offering to You.

SEASONAL DÉCOR TIP It's so fun to keep an assortment of candy canes around. They are inexpensive and can be broken up to use in cookies and desserts or even as a crunchy layer topping the whipped cream on a hot chocolate. Another great idea: hang them from your Christmas tree as ornaments. They are super cute hanging on a tree. Children can easily maneuver a hook over a branch without wielding too much power. So grab some candy canes and keep them on hand!

MINTY FRESH

"Woe to you, scribes and Pharisees, hypocrites! For you tithe mint and dill and cumin and have neglected the weightier matters of the law: justice and mercy and faithfulness. These you ought to have done, without neglecting the others."

<small>MATTHEW 23:23 (ESV)</small>

*P*eppermints and candy canes are a staple candy for the holidays. The candy cane has been around such a long time and if tales I've been told are true, they were invented to keep small children still during long church services! Christians have attached meaning to the shape of the cane to remind us of the shepherd's crook, or to turn it upside down to make a J for Jesus. The colors of red and white remind us of His sacrifice.

No matter what you remember about the mints, may we remember what was important to Jesus. We continually read the imperative to love God and to love others. If we are sure to tithe, pray, and attend services when the doors are open, but fail to love God or others, God is displeased! Loving God means fully loving those whom He loves as well. Without love we are just clanging cymbals.

Lord, let me see people the way You see them and love them the same way You love them.

SEASONAL DÉCOR TIP If you purchase a living Christmas tree, be sure to gather up the extra greenery cut off the bottom. You can even ask if there are additional greenery scraps and branches they'd be willing to give you. You can use this free greenery in wreaths, garlands, and other fresh arrangements that last throughout the season.

EVERGREENS & ETERNAL LIFE

"That whoever believes in Him may have eternal life. For God so loved the world that he gave his one and only Son, that whoever believes in him shall not perish but have eternal life."

JOHN 3:15-16 (ESV)

The birth of Jesus carried the beautiful promise of everlasting life. While we celebrate the miracle of the birth of Christ, as believers, we look ahead to the cross and Resurrection, where we find the true gift of forgiveness of our sins and everlasting life.

Using evergreens in our decorating for the Christmas season makes sense and has become common. Evergreen trees and branches are easy to gather to use in our tablescapes, wreaths, mantels, and more. As their name implies, they stay green and lush for some time after being cut. They are easy to gather, even when conditions are less than forgiving. Having a source of greenery no matter the season helps add dimension and texture to our decorating. Evergreens remind us that everlasting life is possible because Jesus humbled Himself to be born as a man, sacrificed Himself as our atonement, and was resurrected just as He promised.

Lord, I praise You for the reminder of the evergreens. Help me to continue working to accomplish Your work in my life until it's my time to come home.

SEASONAL DÉCOR TIP

Make decorating the tree a family event. Schedule time when everyone is together and enjoy pulling out the ornaments you've collected throughout the years. If you have really breakable items that you don't want little ones to touch, wait until they have put their treasures on the tree and then place the delicate ones by yourself later.

UNCHANGEABLE

"Every good gift and every perfect gift is from above, and cometh down from the Father of lights, with whom is no variableness, neither shadow of turning."

JAMES 1:17 (KJV)

*O*ur traditional Christmas décor revolves around the decorating of the Christmas tree.

Whether the tree is artificial or real, traditional or modern, decorating it is a big part of the festivities in our homes each Christmas. The evergreen fir remains green year-round. Its consistent color makes it a dependable choice for a tree that can be found during any season.

This characteristic of the Christmas tree reminds us that our great God is everlasting and eternal. In a world of constantly changing beliefs, economics, and politics, it's such a comfort to know the One Who doesn't change. He doesn't waver or wonder; He's the only One Who is the same from everlasting to everlasting. While many try to keep up with the shifting sands around us, it fills me with peace and joy to know I can rest in the everlasting character of our God.

Lord, I praise You for Your unchangeable character.
You are the same yesterday, today, and forever.

SEASONAL DÉCOR TIP Always buy more lights than you think you'll need! The end-of-season sales are the best time to stock up on new or different lighting choices. With today's technology there are tremendous advancements in the styles available!

FULL OF LIGHT

"No one after lighting a lamp puts it in a cellar or under a basket . . .
so that those who enter may see the light. . . . If then your whole body is full of light,
having no part dark, it will be wholly bright."

LUKE 11:33, 36 (ESV)

I love a Christmas tree full of lights. There is nothing more disappointing than running out of Christmas lights at the bottom of the tree and having to rearrange the carefully laid strands to extend them further to reach the plug. This year, my family used the copper wired fairy lights to decorate the tree and it was stunning! Tons of tiny lights all over the tree—fully illuminated and beautiful.

I love the description in Luke 11. When our whole body is full of light, it will be wholly bright. When we are operating with the Holy Spirit's power inside us, we should be wholly bright. Like a Christmas tree shining bright in all its glory, the Holy Spirit should radiate out of us into the bitter dark world. And the Good News—you will never run out of that power and light!

Father, fill me with Your Holy Spirit power
so that Your light shows through me and out to the dark world around.

SEASONAL DÉCOR

TIP Whether you grab pine cones at a local store or from your yard they make a great accent or craft piece for the holidays. Layer them in a decorative bowl, insert several in your tree or wreath, or you could make a bird feeder with your family—there's no end to the ideas and uses!

CINNAMON PINE CONES

*"I appeal to you therefore, brothers by the mercies of God,
to present your bodies as a living sacrifice, holy and acceptable to God,
which is your spiritual worship."*

ROMANS 12:1 (ESV)

*W*hen my son was younger, he loved the smell of cinnamon pine cones. Some store-bought bags have the added scent of cinnamon. When the pine cones are placed around the house, they add an extra layer of a warm inviting scent. The pine cones are a traditional feature in Christmas décor. They are easy to gather if you live in the right location—you can just go outside since they seem to be everywhere. They add a touch of natural "outdoorsyness," but they also hold a deeper meaning.

See, the pine cone releases its seeds when it falls to the ground from the tree and eventually dies. Because it releases its seeds, a new tree can grow and pretty soon there are a whole lot of fir trees around!

Paul reminds us in Romans 12:1 that we have to die to ourselves by giving ourselves to God. We become a living sacrifice. Without Christ's death and resurrection, we would have no way of escape or payment for our sins.

*I thank You, Lord, for the powerful reminders
You place around us. Help me to continue to be a living sacrifice for You.*

SEASONAL DÉCOR TIP Another fun way to add the smell of Christmas in your house is to make a stovetop potpourri. Add slices of orange, cinnamon sticks, pine, and cranberries with a cup of water and simmer on low. Replenish water when needed!—Caroline Bivens IG @c.b._designs

carolinebivensdesigns.com

THE THRILL REMAINS

"A woman came with an alabaster flask of ointment of pure nard, very costly, and she broke the flask and poured it over his head."

MARK 14:3 (ESV)

An expensive gift of perfume was given to Christ without hesitation days before the cross, while others exclaimed the gift was frivolous and extravagant. They even asked why she hadn't sold it instead and given the money to the poor! Jesus chided and reminded them that He wouldn't always be with them and to leave her alone because she had done a beautiful thing in her sacrifice.

Do you ever get the desire to give an extravagant gift? I know many people just enjoy giving gifts and others love receiving gifts. I have to admit, I love the opportunity to give a great gift. You know the kind of gift that just surprises someone? You shopped and wrapped the present with love and care, waiting in anticipation to see your loved one open it. It's a special feeling. I can only wonder if this is how Mary felt as she poured the perfume in devotion to Him.

Lord, I pray that my life will be poured out in service
for You for all You have done for me.

SEASONAL TIP During this season consider keeping a few staples in your fridge and pantry. One example is a small wheel of brie. You can make an easy go-to party food in a pinch by slicing off the top and cooking in the oven for twenty minutes with brown sugar sprinkled on the top. Serve with slices of a baguette or a thick cracker.

THE TASTES OF CHRISTMAS

"Oh, taste and see that the Lord is good! Blessed is the man who takes refuge in Him!"

PSALM 34:8 (ESV)

Christmas is a festival for the mouth! The yummy appetizers, cheese trays at parties, decorated cookie exchanges, and festive desserts! The amount of delicious tastes makes for an amazing and fun part of celebrating the season. The length of time we spend in the kitchen cooking and cleaning can add up, but it's such a fun way to interact with our friends and family by sharing in our mutual love of food!

I love how the Bible uses words to paint a picture to help us understand a truth. When I think about favorite Christmas foods, I think about the traditional Christmas turkey and ham. Our family also loves strawberry pretzel salad. It has my favorite flavors and is a delight to eat. I look forward to it and we can't wait to have more. Psalm 34:8 reminds us that we are to delight in the Lord in this same way. By likening it to enjoying our favorite foods, the psalmist gives us a mental image that we can relate to—tasting the delicious foods in mouthwatering pleasure. God desires for us to delight in Him in the same way.

Lord, I delight in You. Help me to always remember
how good You are and how much You love me.

SEASONAL TIP The taste of the food we make varies according to the quality of the items we purchase. In lean years, the choices are simple; we buy what we can afford. When the budget has allowed, though, it has been a treat to purchase a better-quality flour, Mexican/Dominican Republic vanilla, and high-quality cocoa powder. Looking for these specific items on sale does help, as does understanding that you can use less at times of certain ingredients because the flavor is much more powerful.

HEART OF THE HOME

"The good person out of the good treasure of his heart produces good, and the evil person out of his evil treasure produces evil, for out of the abundance of the heart his mouth speaks."

LUKE 6:45 (ESV)

The heart of my family's home is the kitchen. I mean, the way to a man's heart—and let's be honest, mine too—is through his stomach, so the kitchen is prime real estate at our house. Comfort food, family favorites, and healthy choices are all served up in the kitchen. Cookie baking and decorating, desserts, and waffles—you name it—all the good stuff originates here.

Our hearts are no different. The good stuff originates at our core. Or the bad stuff, if that's the case. James reminds us that bitter water and sweet water cannot come from the same location—so if we find the ugliness overflowing from our mouths regularly, we probably need to review what's at our core. What fills us up is overflowing—and if it's not powered by the Holy Spirit, I can guarantee it's going to be distasteful for our families and friends.

*Lord, remind me to keep connected to the Holy Spirit for the power
I need to overflow with love and kindness, especially to my family.*

SEASONAL TIP Having dinner with friends and family in our homes requires an extra bit of work. I prepare as many menu items in advance as possible so I'm able to enjoy time with visiting family and friends.

—Pamela Saumure,
IG @pamela.saumure

DINING TABLE CONVERSATIONS

"Then they told what had happened on the road, and how He was known to them in the breaking of the bread."

LUKE 24:35 (ESV)

*F*amilies bond and friends deepen relationships at the dinner table. Whether it's going out to eat, crashing at a friend's house for takeout pizza, or preparing a meal together—it doesn't really matter. What matters is the time spent talking, joking, and yes, sometimes even arguing. It's no wonder the Bible speaks of the disciples and the early church sitting and fellowshipping over a meal together. It's the opportunity to open up and connect to each other. In many cultures it's still a very revered and valued time. Unfortunately, many of us live in the constant "Go! Go! Go!" and a family meal or dinner with friends is rare. My family's been there—honestly, there are still some days we try to be intentional to lock down times for us to eat dinner together while looking at each other across the table.

Just as Jesus sat and conversed with the disciples, I hope we will learn to value the gift it is to sit with our families or friends over a meal to eat and listen and speak truth. God is with us in all of it—even here at the table.

Thank You, Lord, for the simplicity of the lesson of breaking bread together. Thank You for recording it in Scripture for us to learn from.

SEASONAL TIP My friend Christy has a genius move for decorating gingerbread houses: hot glue their pieces together. Since no one eats the final product, this makes it easier and tons more fun to decorate. Isn't she smart!

GINGERBREAD HOUSES & SHIFTING SANDS

"Everyone then who hears these words of mine and does them will be like a wise man who built his house on the rock. And the rain fell, and the floods came, and the winds blew and beat on that house, but it did not fall, because it had been founded on the rock. And everyone who hears these words of mine and does not do them will be like a foolish man who built his house on the sand. And the rain fell, and the floods came, and the winds blew and beat against that house, and it fell, and great was the fall of it."

MATTHEW 7:24-28 (ESV)

We have decorated more than a few gingerbread houses in my family. It always looks so easy. Unfortunately, I always have trouble creating a sturdy foundation. The whole thing gets assembled only to fall. Eventually it's just a messy nightmare.

Chances are if you grew up in church you remember singing the little song that went along with this passage. It reminds me about the foundations of our lives. If we build on the shifting sands of culture and society, it won't matter how cute and creative the outside looks because the walls are fixing to fall in. By following God's plan and building a strong foundation on His Word and applying it to your life each day, you won't be on shaky ground!

Lord, thank You for the truth of Your Word
and the reminder to build our lives deep in the truth of Your Word.

SEASONAL TIP Bake and decorate cookies, then go deliver them to your family, neighbors, and friends. If you still have more go to the firehouse, police station, and even the nursing home and church staff. Your children not only get the benefit of having made the cookies and the joy of expressing their creativity in the process but also learn the importance of blessing others.

CHRISTMAS COOKIES

*"So when they were sent off, they went down to Antioch, and having gathered
the congregation together, they delivered the letter. And when they had read it,
they rejoiced because of its encouragement."*

<small>ACTS 15:30-31 (ESV)</small>

*W*e read in the Bible that many new believers were discouraged. Church leaders knew how important it was to send them encouragement.

One of our favorite pastimes for the season involves baking and decorating Christmas cookies. I enjoy making snickerdoodles and gingersnaps, but my husband prefers making pressed cookies complete with frosting and decorating! With all that yumminess we tend to eat them all, so I try not to bake too often. Unfortunately, I tend to be much less hospitable when I'm not baking, and that's a terrible thing this time of year. So instead, I still bake the goodies but give them away to friends! Be an encourager and let people know they matter. Everyone could use a kind word and honestly, who wouldn't love a cookie?

*I thank You, Lord, that even Christmas cookies can be used to be a blessing to others
and we can take part in the fun of being that blessing.*

SEASONAL DÉCOR TIP Using old sheet music as part of the décor has come back into style. Roll up a sheet and tie with a ribbon. These can be hung on a tree, paired in an arrangement for a mantle or table with greenery and some small brass instruments, or added to a wreath as an added feature.

THE SOUNDS OF CHRISTMAS

"David also commanded the chiefs of the Levites to appoint their brothers
as the singers who should play loudly on musical instruments,
on harps and lyres and cymbals, to raise sounds of joy."

1 CHRONICLES 15:16 (ESV)

Christmas concerts and recitals start after Thanksgiving and keep going until Christmas Day. A rousing concert of good music celebrating Christmas time is a great way to lift spirits and cheer. As a musician, I've spent gobs of practice time and planning for recitals and performances. We can often hear Handel's "The Messiah," enjoy a beautiful performance of *The Nutcracker*, and hear the bell ringers outside reminding us to be charitable to others.

This passage in 1 Chronicles reminds us of the value that God places on musicians as well. The brothers of the priestly tribe were given the responsibility of being singers who play to raise the sounds of joy. Praise and worship should be a natural part of our lives. We don't have to be good at it to enjoy it. We just need to be cheerful and genuine—raising sounds of joy.

Lord, I thank You for the gift of music and I long to offer it back to You in praise.

SEASONAL DÉCOR TIP Hanging bells on a wreath or door handle adds a festive touch to the seasonal décor. Oversized bells are also a beautiful addition to a mantel.

CHRISTMAS BELLS

"On its hem . . . with bells of gold between them, a golden bell and a pomegranate,
a golden bell and a pomegranate, around the hem of the robe."
EXODUS 28:33-34 (ESV)

My favorite Christmas church services always involve children. One year for the Christmas service, I strung large jingle bells together and let them ring the bells while singing "Christmas Bells." While it was sweet for parents to watch their adorable children on stage, it was even more heartwarming to hear them proclaim the joy of Christ's birth.

Bells are also mentioned in the Bible. In Exodus 28:33-34, the high priests wore golden bells in their garments. The bells would signify to those outside the holy of holies that the priest was still moving around in service to God, and therefore had cleansed himself appropriately prior to entering. Because of Jesus' sacrifice, we no longer need a priest to offer sacrifice for us and we can boldly enter before His throne. I believe we should still be careful to live consecrated and holy lives. As we enter His presence, we should long to have clean hands and pure hearts so that we will be sure He hears us.

Lord, I thank You, most Holy God for the gift of access.
The opportunity to commune with You directly. May I never take it for granted.

SEASONAL TIP Music is an important part of the Christmas season. Playing carols and worship songs will continue to draw our attention to the real reason we celebrate this season.

I WONDER AS I WANDER

"You have taken account of my wanderings; Put my tears in Your bottle. Are they not in Your book?"
PSALM 56:8 (NASB)

*S*ome of my favorite Christmas carols as an adult are not the typical bright cheery fare. Instead, I gravitate toward the more somber and minor tunes like "In the Bleak Midwinter" and "I Wonder as I Wander." Throughout the years, certain songs have connected with me, and not all seasons are easy or joyous, even Christmas. There's still plenty of pain and loss to go around, and unfortunately, the reminders of lost loved ones can be especially difficult to bear during the holiday season. Music connects us emotionally and can help us work through various emotions.

Thinking contemplatively about this season, we can see that even though the birth of Christ was a wonderful occasion, the shadow of the cross loomed. For us, the cross is behind us and we rejoice in its meaning to our salvation, but we can also understand its sorrowful effect on Mary, Joseph, the disciples, and of course God the Father.

What comfort it is for my heart to know that God cares and knows! He knows when we are hurting and when we are struggling, and He is there to comfort us in our sadness.

Thank You for being our Comforter. I rest in Your perfect care
and strength to get me through the difficult days.

SEASONAL DÉCOR TIP As you decorate your tree, add acrylic or glass ornaments that will catch the light. These finishes will do double duty as ornaments and mirrors that reflect light.

—Jennifer Ingram, www.gracious-spaces.net, IG @graciousspaces

PRAISE ON MY LIPS

"An evil man is ensnared in his transgression, but a righteous man sings and rejoices."

PROVERBS 29:6 (ESV)

*W*hether it's the songs that we sing as Christians or the way we stand in line, if the world overhears our conversations, they should recognize something different about me and you. As followers of Jesus, our overall demeanor and disposition should communicate something different to those around us.

Proverbs 29:6 points out to me that a righteous man sings and rejoices. We sing and have joy because we have been given much and have much to celebrate. Unfortunately we live here in the fallen world and experience our share of sorrow and pain, like Jesus did when He was on earth. I fail often, but my desire is that as I long to have Christ fill my mind and heart with His Word, praise will overflow from my lips, and others will recognize my faith by the words that I say and the actions I take. Through my behavior and words, I want strangers to identify that I am one of His.

Christmas is the perfect time to practice this. Each day, I wake with the intention of speaking in love. As the traffic gets heavier, the chaos in stores grows, and the children come home from school for a break, I pray that as the pressures intensify, I will continue to speak in love with joy.

Fill my mouth, dear Lord, with more of You and less of me.
Help me speak words of love, patience, and joy.

Comfort & Joy

COMFORT & JOY

"Then I will go to the altar of God, to God my exceeding joy,
and I will praise You with the lyre, O God, my God."

PSALM 43:4 (ESV)

The chorus of "God Rest Ye Merry, Gentlemen" repeats the phrase "Tidings of comfort and joy." It's interesting that these two ideas are paired together, isn't it? Jesus is many times referred to as our Comforter, the consolation we long for. He is the One who carries our burdens, binds our wounds, and carries our tears. And because He is our comfort, we have joy. Exceeding joy—abundant and overflowing! Not just enough, but more, surpassing our expectations.

Singing Christmas carols and playing them in your home is an important part of the season. Many of the traditional carols we sing are rich with truth. These songs are important because music helps impart these spiritual truths and remind us what we already know to be true, but sometimes forget in the busyness. It adds Christmas spirit and a sense of worship when we sing these songs to the Lord. Think about the words and their meanings and be encouraged!

Lord, I thank You for the gift of music and the carols that we sing today
that remind us of the comfort and joy You bring us!

©beautifullyadorned

SEASONAL DÉCOR TIP You don't have to limit the areas you decorate to just the living room or the area you have a tree. Decorate your entrance, bedroom or porch areas also. Use everyday items as part of your decor, too, like rubber boots, white bark logs, sleds and even ice skates or snow shoes.

INTENTIONAL JOY

"Let the words of my mouth, and the meditation of my heart, be acceptable in thy sight,
O LORD, my Strength, and my Redeemer."

PSALM 19:14 (KJV)

Our minds are fantastic places! We can be doing one thing while thinking about something else. We can be driving and end up at our destination without realizing it. I've practiced a piece of music at the piano while planning out what's for dinner and not really paying attention to the notes I've played. Singing songs can also be the same way. Have you noticed? We can sing a song without really contemplating what the words mean. Unfortunately we can be careless in what we are speaking or saying we will do, instead of being very in tune with what is happening.

I find the same thing true in our lives when we are anxious and fretting. We can be trying to work out world peace, or maybe sibling rivalry, or thinking about lunch after church while singing "How Great Our Joy," but not really meaning or hearing a word of it.

This Christmas let's work to be focused and intentional on what we are singing! Christmas carols are full of good truth and can lead our minds to worship. Let's not miss it!

Lord, I pray that I will set a watch over my lips
and be intentional about the words that I speak— even the ones that I sing.

SEASONAL TIP One of the nice things about the Hallmark movies is that they are usually family friendly. While it's not possible to do every night, it's fun to pop some popcorn, make hot chocolate, and watch a movie together. Make sure to stock up on those fun treats when you are making your menus and enjoy the time with your family and friends.

THE FEEL OF CHRISTMAS

"For the desires of the flesh are against the Spirit, and the desires of the Spirit are against the flesh, for these are opposed to each other, to keep you from doing the things you want to do."

GALATIANS 5:17 (ESV)

'Tis the season of Hallmark movies with virtually the same storyline told by different actors in different locations. While it feels a bit formulaic, who doesn't love the sappy Christmas love stories this time of year? With so much angst and discouragement in the world, having some light, well-meaning fun with a Christmas movie for a few hours sounds perfect.

The challenge for many of us is not to wallow in our emotions. When we let our emotions rule us, our family and friends will not know what to expect from us any given day, and our spiritual life will stagnate. You may have great intentions, but I can promise you: spiritual discipline and emotions won't mix. I won't feel like getting up early to read my Bible, spending extra time memorizing Scripture, or praying over a list of requests. Rather, when ruled by my emotions, I feel like staying in my bed an extra thirty minutes instead!

Father, help me remember that my feelings change often, and my emotions are a terrible gauge of what I should and shouldn't do. Help me remain spirit-filled and controlled.

COZY COMFORT

"Blessed be the God and Father of our Lord Jesus Christ, the Father of mercies and God of all comfort, who comforts us in all our affliction, so that we may be able to comfort those who are in any affliction, with the comfort with which we ourselves are comforted by God."

II CORINTHIANS 1:3-4 (ESV)

*T*he Comforter is His name. In moments of great trial and sadness, we seek comfort from Him Who is already there and knows and understands our deepest pains. Finding rest in Him and with Him helps us to continue on keeping on even when the trial looms long.

In the Northern Hemisphere, Christmas is dominated by the need for cozy styles! It can be cold and sometimes snowy. Thick chunky blankets, flannel pajamas, and hot cocoa create the perfect fireside scene. Home should be the place we rest, relax, and recuperate. Home is the place we can come away to escape the harshness of a bitter world. It's a place for our friends and family. Making our house a home involves a certain amount of cozy comfort. This Christmas let's work on providing not only physical comfort but also emotional comfort to our families and make our home a place we love to come home to.

Thank You for the promise of Your comfort, dear Lord, during seasons of distress.

SEASONAL DÉCOR TIP
A well-lit tree is a beautiful addition to our décor. Consider stringing white lights in the interior of your tree. We often think only to wrap the outer tree, but lighting the inside is the single most effective way to create an eye-catching glow.

—Jennifer Ingram
www.gracious
_spaces.net, IG
@graciousspaces

SON-LIGHT & VITAMIN D

"But if we walk in the light, as He is in the light, we have fellowship with one another, and the blood of Jesus His Son cleanses us from all sin."

I JOHN 1:7 (ESV)

One of the trials of leaving the Florida coast and moving north to Mississippi was the loss of regular doses of sunshine and vitamin D. When you've lived in Florida most of your life, you have no idea what it's really like outside of the state in winter and just how much it affects your mood. I have learned in the last ten years that the lack of exposure to sunlight can drain me physically and emotionally.

My mood is also greatly and to a much larger degree affected by the lack of my direct exposure to the *Son light* as well. When my attitude doesn't square up with living a life filled with the Holy Spirit, I don't need to look far to recognize why. A lack of daily sustenance from the truth of God's Word reveals that sin dulls my shine. When I'm walking in His way and in His Word, the light shines forth.

This Christmas season be sure you're enjoying the *Son light*, and when there's a break in the rain and snow—enjoy the SUNLIGHT as well!

Lord, I thank You for the light of both the sun and Your Son.
Help me to walk closely to You so that Your light shines out from me!

THE SIGHTS OF CHRISTMAS

"Let your light shine before men in such a way that they may see your good works and glorify Your Father Who is in heaven."

MATTHEW 5:16 (NASB)

Certain things just scream Christmas to us when we see them—fir trees, snow, and Christmas lights. My family works hard each year to add a festive touch to our yard. Over the years, we've added a large Merry Christmas sign, colored lights that run along our fence posts, trees wrapped in lights, and more. Yes, it takes time and energy, but we want to celebrate the joy of the season. You can tell we celebrate Jesus' birth at our home based on the décor we put outside. This truth convicts me as I wonder, when people catch sight of me, do they immediately think I am a Christian? When I open my mouth to speak, do I confirm or deny that assumption? Do I look, talk, and react differently than everyone else? Am I attracting people so they want to know me and in turn know my God? If not, I need to reevaluate my choices. My life—every aspect of it—should speak words of affirmation to what I actually say with my mouth and lead others to Christ.

Father, help me to continually bend my will to Yours, and in so doing line up my life to reflect more of You to a seeking world around me. May my walk talk louder than my talk!

SEASONAL DÉCOR TIP Ornaments can be used in a variety of ways, not just on a tree. Hang ornaments and greenery at different lengths from a hanging chandelier or candelabra. This is a great way to vary color schemes, too, if you have some ornaments you love, but have left off because they don't match your tree this year. Now, they can be repurposed for another room.

SYMBOLS

"Tell them to make tassels on the corners of their garments. . . . And it shall be a tassel for you to look at and remember all the commandments of the LORD, to do them, not to follow after your own heart and your own eyes."

NUMBERS 15:37-39 (ESV)

As we study different aspects of the Christmas story, traditions, and symbols, I am reminded that our brains have been wired in such a wonderful way by our Creator. He created us with the ability to tie memory to our senses, and we instantly access a memory deep in the recesses of our minds. Based on the same idea, God commanded the Jewish people to use tassels on their garments. He was very specific in this request because He wanted the symbol to remind them about God's commandments and the need to follow them. He knew their minds were prone to wander and having that visual reminder on their clothing would be helpful.

We decorate for Christmas today without realizing how much the symbols point to the truth of the Spirit. Evergreen trees, pine cones, and bright lights can all remind us about the truth of God's Word and cause us to remember why we celebrate.

Thank You, Lord, for the importance of reminders to our lives. These symbols connect us to You in a deeper way this Christmas season.

SEASONAL DÉCOR TIP If finding local greenery is impossible for you during the Christmas season, then finding good-quality garland at a discount is your next best option! Take advantage of after-Christmas sales to get the very best pricing of the year and prepare for next year!

HOLLY & BERRIES

"And we have seen and testify that the Father has sent His Son to be the Savior of the world. Whoever confesses that Jesus is the Son of God, God abides in him, and he in God."

1 JOHN 4:14 (ESV)

Traditional Christmas décor relies heavily on the colors red and green. The green looks great in decorations with garland and wreaths that come from the outdoor evergreens. The red provides the bright contrast color that came from the berries in the bushes—many times from holly. We still use holly and berries today as part of many of our decorating styles.

The color of the red berry at Christmas also serves as a reminder of the cross and Jesus' crucifixion. It reminds us of the crown of thorns with sharp edges that was placed on Jesus' head. The joy of the birth of Jesus must be remembered with the certain future of His death on the cross. While the Christmas story is not necessarily one of His death and resurrection, all parts of Jesus' life lead to the ultimate sacrifice that He made for all mankind. Oh what a Savior!

I thank You, Father God, for sending Your Son
to be the Savior of the World! What a precious gift!

SEASONAL DÉCOR TIP

Use poinsettias in varying sizes to finish off your decorating. Keep them moist by dropping in a fresh ice cube or two (depending on the size) each day and don't let them get too cold outside at night.

SEASON'S *Greetings*

CHRISTMAS POINSETTIAS

"Now the God of hope fill you with all joy and peace in believing, that ye may abound in hope, through the power of the Holy Ghost."

ROMANS 15:13 (KJV)

The traditional Christmas flower, the Poinsettia, presents various opportunities to attach symbolism and significance to it's connection to Christ's birth. Some have likened the shape of the flowers and leaves to represent the Star of Bethlehem. In various shades of red, white, pink, and marble, the poinsettia is a sturdy plant that can help finish off the Christmas decorating with a dramatic flourish. Until I was researching for this book, I didn't realize that each variety of the flower had its own name. I even discovered a new named variety called Joy!

This Christmas, my greatest hope for you is to know that joy comes directly from God. He fills us with all joy and peace through the power of the Holy Spirit. I find too many of us feel quite hopeless when it comes to politics, the state of the world, or our homes and finances. Friends, please don't forget the power to live this life can be found in the Holy Spirit working in us to accomplish His will. Today, let's make the world wonder what we are all about—celebrate the joy of the season by abounding in hope.

God, I pray that You will fill me up to overflowing so that others may know the hope that lies in me and that hope can change them too.

SEASONAL DÉCOR TIP People often think that décor needs to be expensive to look good. The truth is it's the details and layers that take something from ordinary to extraordinary. By incorporating different textures such as metals, woods, fabric, and greenery, one can achieve a layered look.

—Arianne Miller, IG @millhousestyle

ORNATE ORNAMENTS

"Your adornment must not be merely external—braiding the hair, and wearing gold jewelry, or putting on dresses; but let it be the hidden person of the heart, with the imperishable quality of a gentle and quiet spirit, which is precious in the sight of God."

I PETER 3:3-4 (NASB)

*B*eautiful ornaments of glass, porcelain, metal, and other materials adorn Christmas trees. Each year there is an ebb and flow in the contrast of simple decorating style versus a more ornate design. And all are beautiful in their own way. Whether you choose hand-blown glass ornaments or unbreakable plastic because of the kids or pets, we usually all put some decorations on the tree.

Peter reminds us that the adornments or ornaments we put on shouldn't just be what everyone can see on the outside. Rather, we need to be careful about the adornments of our hearts. Do you ever cringe when you hear about having a gentle and quiet spirit? I do too, friend! I often miss the mark on being gentle and quiet, so this verse speaks loudly to me. Will you join me this year—as we decorate our trees—to ask the Lord to fill us with His power to have a gentle and quiet spirit?

Heavenly Father, enable me to allow You to fill me with gentleness and quietness and transform me into the person You long for me to be.

SEASONAL DÉCOR TIP Just add lights! This is one of the easiest ways to make your home literally sparkle. It can take any room to the next level. With the availability of so many lighting options for interior décor you can have a lot of fun. In the vignette at left I added fairy lights to frame the scroll and wove them into the garland on the back of the pew.

—Jodie & Julie, the Design Twins www.thedesigntwins.com, IG: @julie.thedesigntwins and @jodie.thedesigntwins

CHRISTMAS LIGHTS

"Do not be grieved, for the joy of the Lord is your strength."
NEHEMIAH 8:10 (NASB)

*T*he worst part about decorating with Christmas lights is when you discover a short in the line or a bulb that is not working anymore. If you have multiple light strands running together it can be impossible to identify the one with the problem. You have to narrow down which set of lights is the problem and then figure out which light has to be replaced or if the whole set has gone bad. This takes time and effort, but it's always worthwhile to find the problem and fix.

In our own lives, we have times when we short-circuit. We let sinful and selfish desires interrupt the flow of the current in our lives, and our light dims, dulls, and eventually burns out. Without careful maintenance we can bring down more than just ourselves. We can hurt our families, neighbors, and churches as well. Having the current flowing—the Holy Spirit in us with the hope of glory and fully operational—will keep our lights burning. This allows us to uplift and encourage the ones we love and the ones who need Him.

Thank You, Lord, for being the source of our strength! Help me stay connected to You.

SEASONAL DÉCOR TIP

Use a mix of faux and real greenery. The fresh pine smells amazing, and you can get branches for a good price or even free at your local hardware store or tree farm.

—Caroline Bivens, IG @c.b._designs

carolinebivensdesigns.com

FRONT DOOR DÉCOR

"Behold, I stand at the door and knock. If anyone hears My voice and opens the door, I will come in to him and eat with him, and he with Me."

Revelations 3:20 (esv)

*M*ost years my front door décor has been a given—a decorated wreath. I vary the colors each year, but the wreath is always a staple. This year has been an exception for many reasons, but suffice to say, we like to change things up from time to time and do things a bit different. So this year has been tough. As a matter of fact, I'm still a bit stumped and working on it today in addition to the writing you are read-ing now. As I think about the front door and the porch area, my goal is to create an area that is welcoming and inviting. I want people to know they are important and welcomed, and I truly believe that the front door can be the catalyst to that welcome.

It reminds me of the Guest who stands at the door of our hearts and knocks. He stands and waits for us to open the door and invite Him in. A heart full of envy, bitterness, and pride won't be a welcoming place, so work must be done—confession of our sinfulness. Friend, if you haven't opened your door to Him, I pray that you will today!

Thank You, Lord, for Your constant call to us and for never growing impatient!

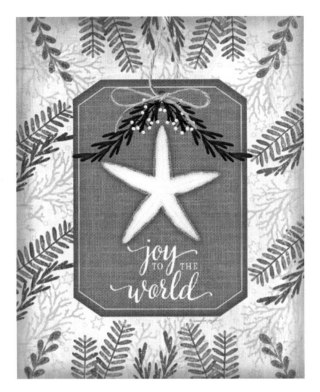

SEASONAL DÉCOR TIP Take advantage of the coastal hues if you live in a temperate climate. Shades of pale blue and green look gorgeous on a Christmas tree, and shells, coral, and driftwood all add a local seasonal flair.

CHRISTMAS DOWN UNDER

"He made the moon to mark the seasons; the sun knows it's time for setting."
PSALM 104:19 (ESV)

During my Bible study this morning I had the opportunity to reflect on God's goodness as the Creator. The chapter above reminded me of His hand in creation and the specificity with which He laid out the changing of seasons. Depending on where you live, your Christmas might not fall in the winter months. Since I live in the United States, it's easy to sometimes forget this truth. We decorate for Christmas in the winter and freeze our fannies off while those of you south of the equator are basking in summer's glow!

I specifically remember my own encounter with Christmas Down Under. Since my mom is Australian, we lived in Brisbane for a few years when I was young. I remember one particular Christmas that was ridiculously hot. Mom had made a beautiful Christmas dinner, but we were all too hot to eat!

Whether hot or cold, the season we are in doesn't really matter. The reason for the celebration, though, remains the same. We celebrate the birth of Christ because He is the promise fulfilled. What a gift to us to have God living and walking among us.

Thank You, Lord, for the reminder that You are in control of it all, even the weather and the seasons.

SHOES OFF, PLEASE

"And the angel of the LORD appeared to him in a flame of fire out of the midst of a bush. He looked, and behold, the bush was burning, yet it was not consumed."

EXODUS 3:2 (ESV)

*T*he Bible tells us it was common practice to remove one's shoes before acts of worship. An example is when God revealed Himself to Moses as holy through the burning bush. Moses acknowledged the barrier between man and God by taking off his shoes and understanding he was standing on holy ground. Because our shoes get dirty when we wear them, the act of removing them represents removing sin from our lives. The presence of sin hinders our ability to worship God effectively. The literal act of removing our shoes to worship symbolizes us coming to our Father in a clean state.

Today, many of us ask our guests to remove their shoes upon entering our homes. We work hard to keep our homes clean and free of allergens. It's a seemingly impossible task, especially during the busy Christmas season! Having to keep dirt and dust from tracking through our homes and staying tidy and orderly can be overwhelming. Any small steps can help—even something as small as removing our shoes.

Lord, I pray You'll bring to my mind unconfessed sins that hinder my ability to worship. I long to keep my sins few and my heart in line with Yours.

SEASONAL DÉCOR TIP LED bulbs allow us greater flexibility in lighting up our décor inside and out. Just be aware that the older technology might not shine as brightly as the more modern LEDs.

ALL IS CALM, ALL IS NOT BRIGHT!

"Abide in Me, and I in you. As the branch cannot bear fruit by itself,
unless it abides in the vine, neither can you, unless you abide in Me."
JOHN 15:4 (ESV)

I was just joking with my husband about some weak bulbs in our Christmas decorations. The LED lights were an older technology and just didn't give off the glow we were both wanting. Kidding around, I told my husband, "All is calm, all is NOT bright!" It didn't strike me until later how much truth was wrapped up in that phrase.

Sometimes life isn't calm, is it? We tend to run to the Lord in those times of need. Life ebbs and flows between difficulty and peace. As it becomes calm again, we tend to depend on God less. We handle life in our own power and control. This is a time that our light doesn't shine bright. We are trying to function without the power of the Holy Spirit and we are less useful for the kingdom. Staying connected requires us to put in the work. Consistently walking with God daily requires effort and intentionality. Don't skip over it, especially in this season when life pulls us in many directions.

Lord, help me to always remember that my source
of strength and power rests solely in You.

North Pole
REINDEER

25 ¢
per ride

SLEIGH RIDES

HOT COCOA, CAROLING
AND WARM BLANKETS

A FAMILY TRADITION

Merry

fir
cedar

spruce
pine

CHRISTMAS

FRESH CUT TREES

SEASONAL TIP Plan into your décor schedule a day designated just for cleaning. No matter the room, a thorough cleaning-out of clutter, dust bunnies, or fallen leaves off the porch will help you start with a clean canvas.

FRONT PORCH DOLDRUMS

"He that covereth his sins shall not prosper: but whoso confesseth and forsaketh them shall have mercy."
PROVERBS 28:13 (KJV)

As we prepare for the Christmas season here in Mississippi, the front porch has taken on a bit of lackluster grimness. Before I can add the touches of Christmas cheer, this must be addressed! Dead plants—from a lack of water or too-cold temperatures, I'm not 100% sure yet—don't look welcoming. Fallen leaves from the surrounding trees are piled in the corners of the porch and need to be swept off. The porch needs to be freshened up before I haul out the Christmas décor and set the stage for the welcome entrance I have envisioned for this year's season.

This accumulation reminds me how my unconfessed sins can sit and clutter up my heart. Unconfessed sin limits the power of the Holy Spirit in my life. No amount of ribbon, greenery, or tinsel can brighten that mess up. Rather a thorough cleaning-out is necessary—just like the front porch needs to be refreshed and cleared of all the junk. It's a reborn area that tells people to come on in—we are ready for you!

Lord, today bring to mind any unconfessed sins that I need to remove from my life. I thank You for the promise of forgiveness if I will but confess and forsake!

SEASONAL TIP As part of your décor prep this year consider making a purchase of some special note cards just for writing a quick note. Or if you are feeling crafty, grab some fresh kraft paper, ink pad, and a rubber stamp to decorate and write a quick personalized note to someone.

WEARY WINTER

"Like cold water to a thirsty soul, so is good news from a far country."
PROVERBS 25:25 (ESV)

*W*inter of the soul is much like winter the season: dreary and dried up. The transition from a cold outdoors to a warm home dries out our hands and lips, leaving us parched. My soul can become dried out too. Even when I'm walking daily in God's Word, sometimes it's just a dry season. Sometimes we just wrestle out the words, or fight our limitations over time or resources. In those seasons, we need a word of encouragement to make it to the goal line.

Don't discount the value of a kind word or email. A handwritten letter or phone call can make a huge impact on someone's life. If someone is in the midst of a difficult time, or under great pressure, taking the time to connect can do an incredible amount of good.

Christmas is such an easy time to do this. Many of us have a few extra hours of downtime and could sit and quickly send an encouraging word to someone the Lord lays on your heart. A gift isn't necessarily wrapped with ribbon and a bow; sometimes it's the words we take the time to say.

Thank You, Lord, for the way You impress on others to speak empowering and encouraging words into my life. Help me to do the same for those around me.

BLUE CHRISTMAS

"A glad heart makes a cheerful face, but by sorrow of heart the spirit is crushed."
PROVERBS 15:13 (ESV)

Color trends vary in popularity each Christmas. The traditional red and green will always remain a strong favorite, but the shades and varieties of other colors provide interest each year as well. One of the trends I love is the blue Christmas tree. While many shades of blue can adorn a tree, a more traditional use of the color blue in its darker hues looks beautiful when paired with silver or even gold.

Unfortunately, a blue Christmas can also mean something entirely different. Many hearts break during the Christmas season. Great loss causes us to struggle during a time when family togetherness is prevalent. The loss of loved ones through tragedy or illness can hit especially hard during this season, and these reminders leave sadness and even depression.

I am reminded that Jesus, the Savior of all mankind, is also my friend who sticks closer than a brother. He cares and sees, and He doesn't miss a single heartache or sad feeling. My friend, if you are struggling during this time, be comforted. He knows just what you are going through and just what you need. He will sustain and comfort you.

My heart aches, Oh Lord, for those who need special comfort. While others celebrate, some remain sorrowful. Please Lord be near to them and comfort them.

©beautifullyadorned

SEASONAL DÉCOR TIP When decorating your tree, place frosted or snowy, long stems along the top of the tree or throughout the tree for a bright, dramatic effect.

—Jennifer Ingram www.gracious-spaces.net, IG @graciousspaces

CHOOSE JOY

"Rejoice in the Lord always; again I will say, rejoice."
PHILIPPIANS 4:4 (NASB)

A fruit of the spirit and a choice, joy is something that Scripture commands. Choosing not to live according to our fleshly desires and emotions, we have the ability through the Holy Spirit to be joyful. In a season that's literally about joy, that should be rather simple, right? Not so much.

In all honesty, the together time that we experience during this season is wonderful, but it can be difficult. It's special to have friends and family from near and far come together, whether it's been a long time or not. The holidays are a fun time of gathering. But there are still challenges. Space is invaded, feelings are hurt, expectations are unmet—it can be a colossal chaotic mess if we aren't careful to choose joy. I recently saw a meme that said, "If you choose not to find joy in the snow, you will have less joy in your life but still the same amount of snow." How true is that?

Maybe you've had a lot of snow, too much family or not enough. Whatever the case may be, you can choose to find joy because the circumstances we find ourselves in are not likely to change.

In the times when I'm feeling overwhelmed, I pray that You'll remind me, Lord, to remain joyful as I allow the Holy Spirit to do His work in me.

SEASONAL DÉCOR TIP

Experiment with different kinds of lighting. Branches and twigs, garland, and more—the possibilities are endless! Curtain lights are beautiful along a wall, or even down a staircase banister for dramatic effect.

LIGHT OF THE WORLD

"Then spake Jesus again unto them, saying, 'I am the light of the world: he that followeth Me shall not walk in darkness, but shall have the light of life.'"

JOHN 8:12 (KJV)

One of the names of Jesus that fits well this Christmas season is the Light of the World. Light naturally draws people in while darkness repels. In the midst of a very dark world, Jesus is a beautiful stark contrast. Part of our distinctiveness as Christians should be the contrast we provide with the world. Being light in a dark world is part of our purpose as Christ followers, and we do that by always drawing attention and bringing glory to His name.

At my house we love to decorate with light. The various shades of light can influence how we feel—warm or cold, energized or relaxed. Advancements in lighting have made it easy to decorate with strings of lights in battery-powered wireless settings as well as traditionally plugged-in cords. The styles and shades of lights vary dramatically and can fit any style of décor. Spilling additional light into our homes is definitely a must-do!

Lord, I thank You for being the Light of the World. I pray that You will use me to give clear testimony of the difference You have made in my life.

SEASONAL DÉCOR TIP In order to have Christmas presents under the tree during the entire season I have faux presents that are just empty boxes wrapped for looks!

—Caroline Bivens, IG @c.b._designs carolinebivens designs.com

THE ULTIMATE GIFT GIVER

"Now there are varieties of gifts, but the same Spirit . . . to each is given the manifestation of the Spirit for the common good."

I CORINTHIANS 12:4-7 (NASB)

*P*rior to Christmas each year as a child, I remember picking through the toy catalog and dog-earing the page corners of the toys I thought I wanted. I always picked out the first things I knew I wanted, but then it seemed I found quite a few other toys I didn't know existed and then I wanted them too!

As Christians, we all have gifts given to us by the Holy Spirit—empowered gifts He gives us to use to accomplish His purposes. I have to be honest and admit that sometimes I wish I had different gifts. While I have a natural desire to teach, I don't always see when others have needs. My skills don't rest in the "helper" category. Sometimes I regret that and wish God had seen fit to give me more in that department! When I am tired and frustrated, I recognize that I'm usually operating outside of what God has designed for me. I'm usually not acting using His power, but I'm in my own flesh instead, acting out my will. I need to trust the Ultimate Gift Giver with the gifts He has entrusted me and work to please Him and bring Him glory by using my gifts and talents to my fullest potential.

Lord, thank You for making me, me. Help me to operate in Your power to accomplish Your work in me!

for unto you is
born this day
in the city of David
a Saviour, which is
CHRIST THE
LORD
Luke 2:11

SEASONAL DÉCOR TIP I keep a consistent decorating theme in a living room by decorating the mantels first and then the trees. This complements the décor of the room.

—Pamela Saumure, IG @pamela.saumure

HOPE BRINGING JOY

"The hope of the righteous brings joy, but the expectation of the wicked will perish."
PROVERBS 10:28 (ESV)

*T*here's nothing quite as sad as being hopeless. When the day starts rough, I burned the bread, the car won't start, and the kids hate me—it's easy to feel hopeless, but I know that a bad day isn't a bad life. I have the hope that going to bed and getting up in the morning will make everything better! Thankfully, it usually does! Proverbs 10:28 reminds me that as we continue to dwell in hope, it will bring us joy. A great opportunity to dwell in hope is the Christmas Story of Christ's birth.

Our hope—Jesus—was born, lived, died, and rose again. Just as it was foretold by the prophets and just as He taught His disciples and crowds of spectators, it would be. Everything came true. All of it. Jesus fulfilled the promise, and because of that I have hope. Hope that this life with its burnt bread, car problems, and teenagers is not all we were made for. I have a future secured because love came down and hope brought us joy.

*Lord, I thank You for the hope that I have because of Who You are.
Thank You for the joy You give!*

SEASONAL DÉCOR TIP Don't be afraid. Make your home and décor your own. It is wonderful that we have so many resources at our fingertips to find inspiration, and there's nothing wrong with finding something we like and doing it but making it your own. Don't copy someone else's style exactly. Do something that shows your own touch. Your personality. Own it.

—Jenny Scholten IG @scholten_family_ceo

THE CHRISTIAN LIVING CONUNDRUM

"Count it all joy, my brothers, when you meet trials of various kinds."

JAMES 1:2 (ESV)

*P*aul teaches us to count it ALL joy—even in the worst of circumstances. Joy in the middle of the difficulty. Joy not just in spite of the trial, but because of it. I don't know about you, but I don't necessarily look forward to difficulty. Physical, spiritual or financial, I try to avoid conflicts and struggles at all costs.

Christmas is a season of joy, but sometimes the trials loom large too. Physical demands on our bodies sometimes cause illness, which means a loss of time with family and friends, gatherings, or decorating. Financial challenges make Christmas gift-giving difficult and they can be a major guilt inducer when we cannot do what we want to do for our families and friends. The spiritual battles can be difficult during this season as we long to do well and live above, but many times we are overwhelmed with busyness—tossed to and fro from one activity to the next. Mentally, many struggle with depression, grief, or loneliness during this time of year. So in this season, let's recognize that our weakness always gives Him a chance to receive all the glory, and our trials build our character and long-term joy.

Lord, may I count it all joy because You sustain me through it all!

SEASONAL DÉCOR TIP Decorating with layers adds interest without adding clutter. So instead of grouping items side by side, try stacking them. We stacked a frame, a charger, and a wreath topped off with a small tree in the center as the main focus of our tablescape. Thereby turning four décor items into one lovely vignette.

—Brandy Bell,
www.sobellandco.com
IG @sobellandco

HYGGE YOUR HEART

"So that Christ may dwell in your hearts through faith—that you, being rooted and grounded in love, may have strength to comprehend with all the saints what is the breadth and length and height and depth, and to know the love of Christ that surpasses knowledge, that you may be filled with all the fullness of God."

EPHESIANS 3:17-19 (ESV)

*H*aving a bedroom that's hygge (hue-geh) during the holidays is essential for my well-being. The Danish word references feeling cozy and special. Unfortunately, it takes constant effort to maintain our bedroom. My tendency when life is busy is to stuff our bedroom with the extra clutter and close the door. This season, I'm working hard to be intentional to keep the clutter to a minimum. The busier the schedule, the more it's necessary to have a place to rest. A candle, a cozy blanket, soft light, and a few moments in God's Word can be all that's needed to recharge after a busy day.

When we prepare our heart, in a hygge manner, we have done all the prep work for our guest (Jesus) to feel comfortable. We've removed the clutter (sin) and set aside time to visit with our guest. When Christ dwells in our hearts, we will know in our deepest core the deep love of Christ.

*Lord, help me to be intentional to keep the clutter
of sin from interrupting my relationship with You.*

UNFAILING, NEVER ENDING

"For I am persuaded, that neither death, nor life, nor angels, nor principalities, nor powers, nor things present, nor things to come, Nor height, nor depth, nor any other creature, shall be able to separate us from the love of God, which is in Christ Jesus our Lord."

ROMANS 8:38-39 (KJV)

*U*sing geometric shapes in our decorating styles helps add texture and flow. Varying sizes of the same shape help to bring symmetry and order to our designs. During the Christmas season we see a lot of circles. Whether it's with a wreath, a candle ring, or an ornament, the circle shape is a great reminder of eternal life and unfailing love.

The promise of unfailing love is such a beautiful comfort. A complete understanding that absolutely nothing can separate us from Christ's love for us changes how we live our lives. Peace characterizes the life of a believer who recognizes this truth. Overwhelming gratitude and joy should also flow out of us when we realize nothing can separate us from the love of God.

Lord, I praise You for the promise of Your unfailing and never-ending love. Thank You for the comfort this brings me during life's most difficult trials.

SEASONAL DÉCOR TIP Our Christmas trees don't need to have perfectly matching ornaments if we don't want them. Some people do, and it looks so beautiful. I truly love seeing that. But for me, my favorite ornaments are the handmade ones from my kids. I am so proud to display them year after year, and the memories they hold are precious. And don't overthink decorations. If you like it, display it. Don't wonder if other people will like it. It's your home.

—Jenny Scholten IG @scholten_family_ceo

HOW GREAT OUR JOY

"Fear not: for, behold, I bring you good tidings of great joy."
LUKE 2:10 (KJV)

*G*ood tidings of great joy—the Messiah was born. Foretold by the prophets of old, the babe had come and fulfilled the first of many promises to Israel.

Uncontained joy fills us and bubbles out to others. Joy marks the presence of a believer. Joy in us is the hope of glory. You see, my friends, joy is the product of hope. It is not batted around by every wind of change. We can be filled with confidence that while today might not be perfect, our hope of eternity—of the surety of our salvation—guides us to look confidently into the future without fear.

It's easy during the busy days of this season to disconnect from joy. Happiness is fleeting, and the to-do list long! We are short on sleep, lacking patience, and snappy with those we love. We start trying to just survive the holidays instead of really dwelling with the joy of the season. Don't allow this to happen! Determine to give yourself space to refocus when life gets overwhelming.

Lord, use me to push others toward You because of the overflow of joy from my life. May I always be a willing vessel.

SEASONAL TIP This season can bring many financial burdens. These burdens only increase under the weight of longing to do more for our dearest friends and loved ones. Let's value the presence versus the presents this season. Give gifts with great love and less debt!

OVERWHELMED WITH AWE

"And Joshua fell on his face to the earth, and did worship, and said unto him, What saith my Lord unto his servant? And the captain of the LORD's host said unto Joshua, Loose thy shoe from off thy foot; for the place whereon thou standest is holy. And Joshua did so."

JOSHUA 5:14-15 (KJV)

*W*hen the Lord appeared to Joshua, he knew immediately who He was, and Joshua's immediate response was worship.

In Matthew Henry's commentary of the Bible he shares, "To Abraham he appeared as a traveler; to Joshua as a man of war. Christ will be to his people what their faith needs." The appearance of Christ as a warrior encouraged Joshua in the battles he was facing. What a beautiful picture of God to us as well. He meets our needs and strengthens us in our weakness.

This Christmas I pray that you will lean into the knowledge that He is sufficient for your every need. The Lord supplies us our needs and gives us encouragement. He is worthy of our worship and adoration!

Dear Father, I praise You for Your amazing grace and meeting us right where we need You. I worship You with all that I am.

Retro-style paper lanterns, paper flowers, and more can all be dropped at various lengths from the ceiling of a room or entrance. These additions add pop to previously unused space and a little bit of awe and wonder too.

MARTHA

"But Martha was cumbered about much serving. . . . And Jesus answered and said unto her, 'Martha, Martha, thou art careful and troubled about many things: But one thing is needful.'"

LUKE 10:40-42 (KJV)

*L*et me start by saying, I know Martha has no part in the Christmas story. I know. But can you imagine Martha at Christmastime, especially in our Western culture? I can—absolutely—because it's me!

I don't say it as a badge of honor either. It's definitely a weakness that when stress hits, schedules cram, and routines topple, I get a little nuts. My fleshly self struggles to be where I'm supposed to be, do what I'm supposed to do, decorate, wrap, smile, take the picture, run the errand, cook the dinner, fold the laundry, and don't forget to smile! I could go on, and I hope you might relate to those struggles too.

I recognize Martha because I see myself. Sister, what would it be like to just lay it all down? All of it. The expectations. The plans. The to-do lists. What if we were just present, in the moment, taking it all in? I don't want to look back and wish I had stopped a little bit more to enjoy life. Join me?

Because life is a vapor, Lord, remind me to take a deep breath in this busy time and to do all I can and then simply enjoy the reason for the celebration.

SEASONAL TIP A journal and nice pen, an app on your phone, and pieces of scrap paper to go into a jar are excellent ways to keep recounting the things we are grateful for. Do this for yourself and then share with your family why you are thankful. This attitude is a great one for them to "catch" from your example.

ATTITUDE OF GRATITUDE

"And let the peace of Christ rule in your hearts, to which indeed you were called in one body. And be thankful."

COLOSSIANS 3:15 (NASB)

*I*t's easy in this season of giving to get caught up in excess. Excess food, excess purchases, and excess attitudes. Instead of being ruled by peace, we are run by chaos and stress, which I believe has its roots in an unthankful spirit. Choosing to be thankful is important during this season. Shopping for bargains on Black Friday can cause us to forget the lessons in gratitude we were just dwelling on during our Thanksgiving meal. Stopping to assess our heart's condition is essential during this season. Being intentionally thankful is the key to seeing the peace of Christ rule in us.

Journaling can be such a beneficial way of connecting our minds with gratitude. Writing in a gratitude journal can remind us of something good we've experienced. Despite good intentions, it's rare we remember all the good stuff that happens day to day. It doesn't matter if it feels mundane because, honestly, keeping a conscientious record of the God things that are happening in your life makes for great reading when you are discouraged or defeated.

Lord, help me to be purposeful in recounting my benefits.
Let me have an attitude of gratitude during this busy Christmas season.

SEASONAL DÉCOR

TIP Add real or faux cotton-like ornaments throughout your tree. You'll love the farmhouse feel and billowy texture that cotton adds! This will add a light, bright feel full of texture and dimension!

—Jennifer Ingram
www.gracious-spaces.net,
IG @graciousspaces

there's nothing like a farmhouse Christmas

FULLNESS

"For from His fullness we have all received grace upon grace."
JOHN 1:16 (ESV)

The word "fullness" in John 1:16 derives its meaning from the Greek word pleroma, which means a filling supply and is used in the context of completing an incomplete thing or filling an empty supply. Other verses in the New Testament use this word to explain the fullness of God in Jesus. We understand that He was fully God and fully man. This truth, though, is difficult for the human mind to understand. The truth of Scripture is that Jesus lived His life on earth fully God and fully man and out of that fullness, He offers us grace. Fullness implies an abundant supply. His fullness comes from an abundant supply of God. From this abundant supply, we receive grace upon grace.

An abundant supply of grace is necessary to survive the difficulties of this life. For ourselves and others we deal with on a daily basis, grace is necessary to both give and receive. I rejoice for the connection to the Source of this fullness of grace.

Father, I thank You for Your grace, Your unmerited favor, in my life.
Thank You for providing that grace abundantly. May I return that grace to others!

SEASONAL DÉCOR TIP Consider the Jesse Tree in your decorating this season. Helping our children connect their understanding of the Bible directly to Jesus' birth can impact them for life. Jesse trees can be small trees, real or faux, or even simple branches hung on a wall.

CELEBRATING THE TRADITIONS
OF THE SEASON

"There shall come forth a shoot from the stump of Jesse, and a branch from his roots shall bear fruit."

ISAIAH 11:1 (ESV)

*F*amilies celebrate the season in a variety of ways. Depending on your religious background and your culture, you may have some special activities you do each year as your traditions. Many of the traditions celebrated today have been around for hundreds of years. One that I've seen celebrated incorporates daily readings of Scripture from Creation to Christmas. The Jesse Tree is named for the father of King David. Jesus was a descendant of King David and fulfilled one of the Old Testament promises: that David's bloodline would always rule Israel.

The Jesse tree is easy to do with children because each day an ornament is directly connected to a Bible story and placed on the tree. The telling of the story connects children with the importance of the Christmas season and the Bible. If you find yourself burned out from reminding your children that it's not about the gifts under the tree, perhaps this tradition with its focus on God's word will bring their attention back to the real reason we celebrate.

Lord, I thank You that You came, lived, died, and rose again just as You said.
Thank You that I can share with confidence the truth of Your story.

SEASONAL TIP Every Christmas Eve, we have the same traditional menu. The whole family looks forward to it, this one night of the year, and then after church service, we enjoy a quiet evening watching *It's A Wonderful Life*.

—Pamela Saumure IG @pamela.saumure

JOY SNATCHERS & FOX CATCHERS

"Catch the foxes for us, the little foxes that spoil the vineyards,
for our vineyards are in blossom."
SONG OF SOLOMON 2:15 (ESV)

Have you noticed that it's the little things that build up and steal our joy? I'm not immune to it, either, and have noticed especially this week how easy it is to let them in. The weather, the delivery not being on time, the wrong item being shipped, or the unexpected extra bill at Christmas: so many little things can slip in, pile up, and threaten to steal our joy—making us irritable and unhappy.

The Christmas season always seems so busy. No matter how hard we might try, the little foxes spoil the vine. It's important to recognize this when it happens so we can reject and repair as quickly as possible. We can't always prevent the distractions and discouragements, but we can teach ourselves to recognize when they are happening and work to remove the frustration as quickly as possible so we can remain in the joy that is meant for us.

Lord, help me to recognize the joy snatchers and remove them from my life.
Help me to turn to You for help when I'm struggling.

SEASONAL DÉCOR TIP Have some fun with gifts and wrap them in unique ways. Wrap them in several boxes to make the excitement of unwrapping the gift last a little longer. Plus it will disguise what might otherwise be an obvious gift!

JOY WRAPPED IN UNEXPECTED PACKAGES

"Not only that, but we rejoice in our sufferings, knowing that suffering produces endurance, and endurance produces character, and character produces hope."

ROMANS 5:3-4 (ESV)

Hope and joy are byproducts of trials and struggles in our lives. Suffering producing endurance means welcoming the tests in our lives. While I certainly don't mean to suggest that we ask for the trials to help us to grow our hope and joy, we must recognize that when they come they will produce in us those very things. Just as joy came wrapped in dirty cloths and lying in a manger—a King among the work animals. Unwrapping the gift of joy after suffering can be a painful process because of each prickly layer. Yet, the true gift lies at the core, where the source of joy rests: Christ our Lord!

We don't have joy because our paychecks are fat, our homes are perfect, or our children are well behaved. Rather, joy comes from enduring difficult trials with an eye to a future that is already settled, prepared, and waiting for us. A future that looks nothing like our present or even anything we can imagine and wrap our minds around! True joy is content knowing that no matter what today holds, Jesus has already prepared the very best for us.

Thank You, Lord, for the gift of joy. Though wrapped in pain and struggle we praise You for how You work in us to produce an overflowing joy.

Your color scheme is important and determines your overall mood. After all, color is a powerful element in your festive holiday home theme. Decide if you want to stay more neutral, or traditional red and green, or perhaps use an original color combination. There are endless color schemes for Christmas. Have fun and let your imagination be your guide.

—Jodie & Julie the Design Twins
www.thedesigntwins.com,
IG: @julie.thedesigntwins and
@jodie.thedesigntwins

THE HOLLY & THE IVY

"For Christ also suffered once for sins, the righteous for the unrighteous, that He might bring us to God, being put to death in the flesh but made alive in the spirit."

1 PETER 3:18 (ESV)

With multiple verses to the traditional Christmas carol "The Holly and the Ivy," it's easy to miss the meaning the lyricist intended behind the words written. While many Christmas songs speak of Christ's birth, this one points to the Crucifixion. 1 Peter 3:18 reminds us of Jesus' purpose. The mother and her child, a beautiful picture of love and then grace as she ultimately had to let Him go to the cross. Mary experienced the gift of His presence in her life as she watched Him grow from boy to man, and then as He continued to do the will of the Father. His purpose was not to be her son, but rather to be the sacrifice for all mankind.

Do you ever struggle with your purpose? Or perhaps your struggle is in letting go of your children for their purpose? Our goal as parents should be to raise our children to be all they can be in pursuit of glorifying and honoring God with their lives.

Lord, I thank You for the reminder in this Christmas carol to continue to seek Your purpose not only in my life but also for those who surround me as well!

SEASONAL DÉCOR TIP Consider using words as part of your decorating this season. You can find ornaments, wood/tin cutouts, and wall art featuring different words for the season like Hope, Joy, and Peace. Our world especially needs these reminders today. Hope has come, and He walked among us.

HOPE

"My soul continually remembers it and is bowed down within me. But this I call to mind, and therefore I have hope: The steadfast love of the LORD never ceases; His mercies never come to an end."

LAMENTATIONS 3:20-22

This season brings a great reminder of hope. Hope reminds us that although life is not easy or simple, we can rest in the knowledge of His unending love. His mercies—which are new each morning—and His faithfulness are great. Because we are Christ followers, hope fills our hearts to keep on keeping on. When the trials come—and they do—when the temptations rise—and they will—hope prompts us to rest, knowing that it's all under God's control, that nothing is a surprise to Him.

I love setting out reminders of these simple words each year. We have several silver four-inch ornaments for our tree that say Joy, Peace, and Love. I love these visual reminders available right before my eyes. The Christmas season is the remembrance of the fulfillment of God's promise: the Messiah, our Rescuer, the babe in the manger, the perfect spotless Lamb of God, would take away the sin of the world. This is the hope we all need for a future and for today.

I praise You, Father, for the hope You promise each of us because of the way that You provided for us.

SEASONAL DÉCOR TIP

When decorating your tree consider adding flocking with a simple spray can from Amazon or your local craft store. It's much more cost effective to spray your own and it adds so much beauty. Then add large, white ornaments like snowflakes, not only on the outer branches, but also deeper into the tree to add dimension. Don't be afraid to evenly distribute large ornaments on your tree.

—Jennifer Ingram, www.gracious-spaces.net, IG @graciousspaces

LIMITATIONS BRING PEACE

"Follow peace with all men."
HEBREWS 12:14 (KJV)

Do you find yourself busier than ever with an overcrowded schedule and endless commitments this time of year? It's hard to find the peace that we long for when we are running from one end of the county to the other. We chauffeur the kids to practices and games, Christmas parties and gatherings with friends. Obligations and commitments can zap the peace right out of our hearts. Creating negative space during this time is supremely important.

In our décor, sometimes we find that less is more. We can feel more peaceful when we have less chaos surrounding us. My friend, this means learning to say no. While I'm not the expert here, I do know that learning to say no and setting boundaries is important. After all, He came to bring us peace! Don't you think He means for us to enjoy just that?

*Thank You, Father, for the peace I find in You despite busyness
and packed schedules. Help me learn to set proper boundaries
so that I can remain at peace even when I'm busy.*

SEASONAL TIP
End-of-season sales are a great time to stock up on gifts for next year. You can be kind to your Christmas budget by making discounted purchases after Christmas this season. Even the high-cost ticket items can be drastically reduced during the post-holiday sales. Just don't forget where you hide those Christmas gifts for next year!

GIVER OF GOOD GIFTS

"If you then, who are evil, know how to give good gifts to your children, how much more will your Father Who is in heaven give good things to those who ask Him!"

MATTHEW 7:11 (ESV)

Christmas gifts belong in a category all their own! Gifts are fun to give and receive throughout the year, but no birthday, anniversary, or graduation can compare to Christmas morning! Watching with anticipation as each member of the family opens his or her gifts with surprise and even sometimes shock fills me with such joy. I love to watch their reactions and see if we hit the mark with what we thought they wanted.

Matthew 7:11 resonates deep in me because I know how much I enjoy giving gifts to others. And if my excitement in gift giving is just a tiny sliver of what my Father longs to give me—I can honestly say it blows my mind! How much more He wants and desires to do for us—all we have to do is ask! We forget and talk ourselves out of big dreams and big goals for the Kingdom when He really longs to bless us so that we can in turn bless others and bring Him glory.

I thank You, Lord, that You hear and answer the big and the small requests I have, and I praise You for Your faithfulness to supply my every need.

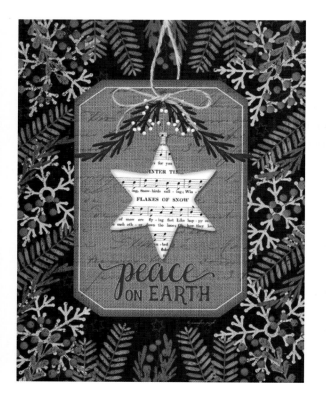

SEASONAL TIP This season let's be looking for those who need help. Maybe a widow has a house project needing a helping hand, a family needs a meal delivered or to be invited to your table with your family, or a single mom could use some extra funds to pay bills and buy her family presents. Ask God to put someone in your path to help. He will surely honor that request!

BEAR EACH OTHER'S BURDENS

"And Judah said, 'The strength of the bearers of burdens is decayed,
and there is much rubbish; so that we are not able to build the wall.'"

NEHEMIAH 4:10 (KJV)

*W*hile we have much to celebrate this season, we don't have to look far to see those who are struggling. A spouse adjusting to life on his or her own, or a family dealing with a grave illness or an unexpected job loss, can hit especially hard during this season. While everyone else is attending gatherings and celebrations, these ones are left with memories of how things used to be. Those memories can hurt more in a season meant for joy, especially if the loss is still fresh.

The Jewish people knew much about mourning their losses. As God's chosen people they squandered so much because of their sin and disobedience. Various stories in the Bible remind us that we are to bear each other's burdens. This passage in Nehemiah 4 emphasizes the need for help in trying to rebuild the wall around Jerusalem. Their strength was weak because the work was great and they required assistance. In this same way, we should be available to assist others doing God's work.

Lord, help me see others in need this season and take action to help.
I want to be a good burden bearer for others.

SEASONAL DÉCOR TIP Have fun! Our homes do not need to be perfectly staged at all times. My favorite Christmas décor is our "Snowball fight" station. My boys LOVE throwing snowballs at each other. It's fun and we end up laughing so hard.

—Jenny Scholten, IG @scholten_family_ceo

JOY TO THE WORLD

"And thou shalt have joy and gladness; and many shall rejoice at His birth.

Christmas is the season of joy, and yet I'm afraid many of us don't understand or even experience joy. One of my favorite quotes about joy comes from Adrian Rogers. He said, "Happiness is like a thermometer; it registers conditions. Joy is like a thermostat; it controls conditions." This passage in Luke 1 illustrates the joy and gladness that were a byproduct of the good news for Zechariah and Elizabeth and their long-awaited child. Keeping lighthearted attitudes and fun at the center of our home during the Christmas season can be challenging when the kids are young and we are so busy. Be sure to look for opportunities to celebrate the joy and happiness the season brings instead of getting wrapped up in the things that distract from the true reason we celebrate—Jesus' birth.

Whether you are experiencing a loss, are in a waiting season, or have unfulfilled needs or desires, you can still walk in the habit of joy as you rest in His sovereignty. I know it can be easy to lose a happy spirit in those seasons, but joy can remain steady because it's rooted in the goodness of God and His will.

Lord, I thank You that You are good and that You do good. May my life express the joy of that knowledge to others around me.

HEART & HOME FOR CHRISTMAS   181

SEASONAL DÉCOR TIP
A lovely feature I've seen lately in decorating with natural outdoor finds is a medium-size tree branch or small tree trunk turned on its side on a wall or in a corner. From here silk ribbons in various lengths can hold ornaments, trinkets, or other hard-to-place decorations.

ALL TANGLED UP

"No soldier gets entangled in civilian pursuits, since his aim is to please the one who enlisted him."

2 TIMOTHY 2:4 (ESV)

*E*ach year I plan for Christmas to be kinder, gentler, and less busy. Yet, each year I find myself struggling with the same laundry list of struggles. Like strings of Christmas lights that are hopelessly entangled no matter how they are stored, I inevitably feel exhausted and overwhelmed at some point.

When I feel like this, it's a good reminder to read the truth in 2 Timothy 2:4. See, we are running a race as the soldiers of Christ. We have a job to do, and Timothy reminds us that to be good soldiers, we cannot engage in civilian pursuits or entanglements. That makes sense to me even though I haven't served any time in the military. I know that anytime we have our eyes on a goal, distraction will keep us from accomplishing it. Even good things can be a distraction, but we are told not to get entangled. My mission is to serve my family and friends with love and joy this season. If I am struggling in this mission, then I've found myself entangled in civilian pursuits and need to remove the distractions from my life. See, my aim is to please the One who enlisted me.

Lord, I pray during this season of busyness that You'll keep me above the noise of distraction.

SEASONAL DÉCOR TIP Not liking the base of the small tree after ordering it, I found a ceramic vase from my bedroom and tucked the tree inside. I styled it with pink ornaments, finishing it off with a pink satin ribbon.

—Kathy Atkins
livebeautifullyadorned.com,
IG @beautifullyadorned

GOOD DIRECTIONS

"For to the one who pleases Him God has given wisdom and knowledge and joy."
ECCLESIASTES 2:26 (ESV)

Don't you hate driving around a new city? Even with GPS and turn-by-turn instructions, I struggle to know how far I have to keep driving before that next left turn comes up. Or I stay in the right lane too long and it's a must-turn lane . . . ugh! It seems we aren't immune to wrong directions at Christmas either. While many travel back to the familiar territory of family homes, others take trips to new destinations. Maybe if you don't travel, you at least may try out a new shopping center or restaurant that you've never been to before. There's always the flurry of things to do during the holiday season, but Ecclesiastes 2:26 reminds me that God alone is the source of wisdom, knowledge, and joy—helping us find our way.

When I don't know what to do next, I can trust that He has all the answers I need. As I walk with Him in obedience, He provides wisdom to make the right decisions. I think joy is added here as the cherry on top. Because when we have wisdom and knowledge, we can rest and not worry about that decision—that truly is joy.

When I don't know what to do, keep my eyes on You.
Let me trust and have joy that You will answer and meet all my needs.

SEASONAL DÉCOR TIP Simplify, simplify, simplify. In our Pinterest and Instagram culture we can feel the constant pressure to be more and to do more. Keep in mind, we don't have to decorate every room of the house to celebrate well. Rather, we need to do what time allows and simplify so our families enjoy our presence and not just presents.

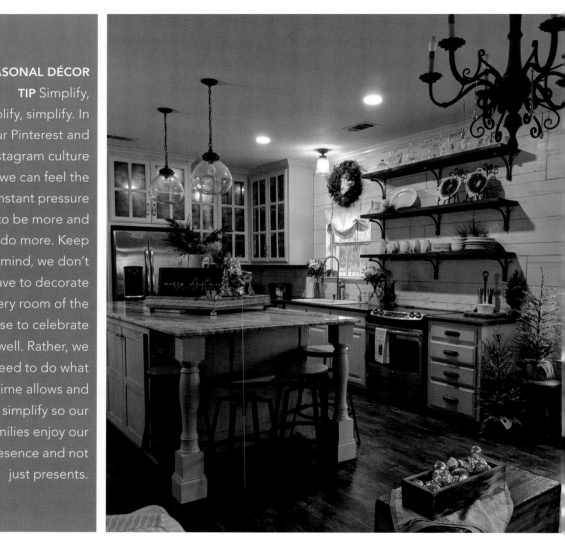

SPIRIT-FILLED SELF-CONTROL

"A man without self-control is like a city broken into and left without walls."
PROVERBS 25:28 (ESV)

Have you noticed that the happiest time of the year is also the "I'm so stressed out I could scream" time of the year? During Christmas, I find the pressure to be under control of my emotions more difficult than normal. It's a challenge when our energy levels run low and it feels like everyone needs a piece of us. Instead, I'm happier when my coffee is hot, my children are nice, and my husband is kind. When these conditions aren't met, I'm not happy. And "when Mama ain't happy, ain't nobody happy." We women tend to have more control of the atmosphere of our home than we realize.

So being in control by the Holy Spirit's power and full of His joy is essential for not only our spiritual condition, but also the condition of those around us whom we love and cherish. Our source of joy is rooted in Christ and the knowledge of what His salvation has already accomplished for us. Because of that steadiness, joy doesn't just come and go. The winds of difficulty, trial, and loss can blow hard on us, but my joy remains.

*Lord, I thank You that You are the rock I can rest upon while
I allow the Spirit to help me control my fickle emotions.*

SEASONAL DÉCOR TIP If you run out of room on your Christmas tree for hanging more ornaments, think outside the box—or the tree, if you will. For instance, place ornaments on the coffee table. When placed on a table in pairs or leaning alone, they complete the look.

—Kathy Atkins
livebeautifullyadorned.com,
IG @beautifullyadorned

IMMANUEL—GOD WITH US

"'Behold, the virgin shall conceive and bear a son, and they shall call His name Immanuel' (which means, God with us)."

MATTHEW 1:23 (ESV)

*M*atthew records the fulfilling of the Old Testament prophecy. Isaiah prophesied that a virgin would conceive and bear a son and call Him Immanuel. His very nature being part of our flesh and walking among us. God with us was the promise, and the fulfillment was that He indeed arrived as a baby and encountered life just as we do on earth. All of it. This promise fulfilled is so comforting because it breaks down the barrier between God and man. Just as His eventual death on the cross tore the curtain in two, God with us brings Him close, touching us in His humanity.

When I struggle and suffer the sorrow of loss, I need only to look to the Gospel to read about Jesus' walk on this earth. It means so much to have a Savior who knows my humanity because He had to walk the walk with our human limitations. There is no one else that can empathize with my struggle like He can. That's the beauty of Immanuel, God with Us.

What a precious gift, dear Lord, of coming and making Your dwelling among us. I thank You for that precious comfort.

SEASONAL DÉCOR TIP As you finish decorating, add colorful ribbon to your tree. Whether you choose long strips that cascade down or smaller strips you tuck inside, ribbon adds soft texture that distributes brightness all over your tree.

—Jennifer Ingram www.gracious-spaces.net, IG @graciousspaces

DEEP ROOTS

"Therefore as you have received Christ Jesus the Lord, so walk in Him,
having been firmly rooted and now being built up in Him and established in your faith,
just as you were instructed, and overflowing with gratitude."

COLOSSIANS 2:6-7 (NASB)

*W*e live just down the road from a Christmas tree farm. It's pretty amazing to watch the transformation over the last few years of the little tiny seedlings that have grown up and grown into the lush Christmas trees many families take home to celebrate the season. They are cared for carefully throughout the year with regular watering, feeding, and trimming. When Thanksgiving comes around, the father and son open their tree farm for several weeks to welcome others to cut down a tree.

In order to face the challenges of life, we need deep roots too. If we intend to live a life worthy of the Gospel, we have to be intentional about the regular watering, feeding, and trimming of our souls. Spiritual disciplines, while sometimes not a favorable topic, are essential! And while living a disciplined life is never easy, it is for our good and His glory.

Father, I pray that You will make me intentional about following You and being consistent in spending time in Your Word being molded by Your truth.

SEASONAL TIP Don't wait until the end of the year to start purchasing gifts for those you love. Keep a journal or take notes on your phone when people mention something they'd like. Then as sales occur throughout the year, you'll be ready to make those buys and be able to give meaningful gifts.

HEART OF WORSHIP

"A woman came up to Him with an alabaster flask of very expensive ointment, and she poured it on His head."
MATTHEW 26:7 (ESV)

*H*aving a heart of worship requires a willingness to sacrifice. Sacrificial worship overflows from our devotion. This reminds me of the woman here in Matthew with the expensive alabaster box filled with luxurious perfume. Not caring what others might think, she broke open the box and spilled out the perfume on Jesus' head in anticipation of his death on the cross and eventual burial. Her gift of reckless abandon was treasured by Jesus because He knew she gave from a heart of worship in adoration of Him.

During this season of gift giving, we can find ourselves paralyzed trying to find just the right gift for the individuals on our list. Many times it's more difficult to find gifts for those we love because we want our gift to be meaningful and special. Giving a thoughtful gift considers their needs, wants, and desires and demonstrates how we feel about that person.

I wonder what we could pour out in our worship of Christ. What precious possession would we be willing to part with and pour out in worship?

Lord, You are the only One worthy of my allegiance and devotion and my deepest admiration.
May I be willing to give all I possess to you in return for all you have done for me.

SEASONAL DÉCOR TIP

Don't be afraid to use items for a different purpose than what they were intended. For instance, I recently need a new white table runner for my dining table but I didn't want to purchase something new. Instead, I grabbed an extra throw that I wasn't using. Folded neatly, it is now a beautiful runner!

—Kathy Atkins
livebeautifullyadorned.com,
IG @beautifullyadorned

RESPONSIBILITY'S BURDEN

"He himself bore our sins in His body on the tree, that we might die to sin and live to righteousness. By His wounds you have been healed."

I PETER 2:24 (ESV)

As I write this book, I sense a tremendous burden of responsibility. Not only do I consider my commitments very seriously, but I also know that the words I write, and the truths I hope to share, require me to rightly divide God's Word. It is a heavy burden because I am most definitely fallible and finite. I don't know it all and I'm still always learning, but I pray that God will use my words in spite of me.

It reminds me of the even greater burden that Christ bore for our sins. See, the beautiful part of the Christmas story isn't the birth of a babe in a manager. It's the life He lived as the Son of God, who eventually died on the cross to bear our sins and rose again on the third day. It's the beauty and horror of it all mixed together into the truth of salvation—the true gift of the Christmas season. The precious, priceless, sacred gift of new life in Christ.

Dear Jesus, I thank You once again for doing what no one else could have done for me. What a beautiful gift You are.

LIMITED

"Teach us to number our days, that we may gain a heart of wisdom."

PSALM 90:12 (NIV)

Twenty-four hours a day, seven days a week for three hundred sixty-five days a year for however long God allows us to live on the earth. We will not live forever and our limitation is something we cannot control. We've been around long enough to know that winter doesn't last forever, and neither does summer. Things eventually change and come to an end. While I'm glad that winter doesn't last any longer than it does, I am usually sad when summer comes to an end.

While we know this reality to be true in Creation, we sometimes forget that we aren't guaranteed a particular number of days. We don't know if we will live to eighty years old or pass away at sixty-five. Yet, we tend to live our lives as if we will always be here on earth. What if instead we switch our perspective and view life as fleeting? Would we be more intentional about spreading the Good News? This is our purpose and reason for living. As we launch into a New Year, let's bear this truth in mind.

Lord, teach me to be intentional with every moment, every day, knowing that it may be my last.

SEASONAL TIP
There is always a bit of downtime between the end of the year and getting back to routines. Allow yourself room to consider the past year. Maybe you don't like to journal or keep a calendar/diary, but you could keep a jar to drop little notes in throughout the year. Big wins, small wins, and special adventures could all be dropped in the jar and are a fun way to review your year!

CELEBRATING ACCOMPLISHMENTS

"The desire accomplished is sweet to the soul."

PROVERBS 13:19 (KJV)

*E*nd-of-year reflection creates opportunity to look back on goals met, goals denied, or goals that may have changed throughout the year. Whether they are physical, mental, or spiritual goals, thinking back through our year helps us determine what we should focus on for the next year.

Reflecting allows us the opportunity to thank the Lord for the way He has worked throughout the year. Many of the blessings we can count are not ones we actually listed on the calendar. The difficulties don't usually land on the planner pages either, but God already knew and already provided the grace needed. Even as I complete this book, I reflect on the opportunities He has used to continue to teach me to rely on Him. I pray that the thoughts you read here will be a blessing to each one who reads because of Him working through me.

I do hope, friend, that you allow yourself time to reflect. Seeing goals met, Christ working in our life, and spending time with family and friends is such a sweet thing. Praise Him!

Lord, I thank You again for the way You work and allow me to join You where You already are. Thank You for making the journey full of sweetness along the way.

There's nothing like fresh paint to brighten a room and give a new perspective. Walls get scuffed and scraped over time, and a fresh coat of paint can brighten not only the room but our whole demeanor as well.

FRESH STARTS & NEW HEARTS

"Brethren, I count not myself to have apprehended: but this one thing I do, forgetting those things which are behind, and reaching forth unto those things which are before, I press toward the mark for the prize of the high calling of God in Christ Jesus."

PHILIPPIANS 3:13-14 (KJV)

There's not much more of a fresh start than a New Year. While we might have some regrets, and desires to do things better in the future, a fresh start provides momentum to really begin again. It's like a brand-new page we get to mark the first lines on as we begin a new year each January 1st.

This is the same thing we must do when we run the race of the Christian life. We must leave the things that are behind us, and we must press on. Failures and successes are both in the rear view—living in the past never helped us move forward into all that the future holds. We must continually press on with God's grace and mercy to accomplish what His purpose is in our lives.

Lord, I thank You for the beginning of a New Year.
I submit my past failures and successes into Your hands and ask
You to make me more like You in the year ahead.

SEASONAL TIP Getting the family together to set vacation plans and back-to-school schedules can be difficult. But this time is well spent because it will also allow you to talk about setting goals with each other. Consider sharing a digital app that communicates with everyone at once. And keep a paper schedule as a backup!

PLANNING A NEW YEAR

"Many are the plans in the mind of a man, but it is the purpose of the Lord that will stand."

PROVERBS 19:21 (ESV)

*C*hances are if you are reading this, you have found yourself in that interesting little time frame between Christmas and the first of the New Year. Days of rest and reflection while schedules are nonexistent are also a perfect time for us to sit and consider what the New Year might hold. With a yearly calendar in hand and a pen and paper (and a hot cup of coffee!), we can sketch out a framework for the coming year. I realize that the year never quite flows as we plan, but having an idea of what we already know will happen helps shape our goals—like bucket-list travel, more time with family, and work responsibilities.

As my mind always loves to dream big and plan way more than I can realistically accomplish, I remind myself of the wisdom found in Proverbs. While we make plans, we also need to be mindful of what God's purpose might be for the year ahead. We should have a healthy balance of big dreams and goals with large doses of prayer asking God to reveal His purpose and plan.

Lord, I thank You for the New Year ahead and pray that I will follow Your purpose for my life as I set goals and schedules.

SEASONAL DÉCOR TIP

Some décor isn't uniquely Christmas in our homes. If you don't want to remove all the Christmas at once, consider leaving out a few select items as your winter design. Many natural décor elements like greenery, twigs, and pine cones are items that can remain past Christmas until we begin decorating for spring!

REFLECTION

"But Mary kept all these things and pondered them in her heart."
LUKE 2:19 (KJV)

I love this verse in Luke 2:19 and I love reflecting. It's part of my nature to sit and think things through by trying to understand what is actually taking place, reflecting on what went right or wrong, or reminiscing on special memories. I love to sit and think, and when I read that Mary stopped and took the time to reflect in the midst of all that was going on around her, I understand I also need to sit and process the events in my life.

This season post-Christmas prompts a natural sense of reflection as well. We think about time gone by, memories made, and start to make plans for a New Year. We think back through what we have done and what we want to do, and then we are off to the races again—back into our daily routine faster than we can blink.

This year, take the time to reflect, to ponder, and to keep these things in your heart. Remember the good that God has done and make a point to thank Him for it.

Father, I thank You for the mighty works You have accomplished in me this year. I praise You with my whole heart.

ACKNOWLEDGEMENTS

*N*o one journeys alone. The path to publication intersects and merges with others along the way to provide us the greatest benefit of knowledge, experience and camaraderie.

I'm thankful for wisdom and insight from the team of Serious Writer Inc. friends who are like family, Bethany Jett, Cody Morehead, and Michelle Medlock Adams, and including my agent Cyle Young of Hartline Literary and Junior Agent Bethany Morehead. I am incredibly grateful for Abingdon Press Acquisition Manager, Karen Longino, who saw the vision for this project and championed it forward through each meeting, believing in this book and including me in so much of the process.

An important part of my story includes my family. My parents, Glen & Jennifer Weeks have always believed that I could do anything I set my mind to. I'm thankful for our children, Kayla, Emma and Connor who have not only had to pick up the slack in the wake of my writing life, but have also cheered me on with enthusiasm. My husband, Rob Duerstock listens to my great big ideas and never shoots them down. He has encouraged my pursuit of the dreams God has given me and for that I will always be grateful.

Lastly because it is of the greatest importance, I am thankful for the Lord's intervention in my life bringing me to salvation, and the ongoing process of sanctification which brings me to this stage in order to write my heart on the page. I am humbled that He would use me in this way.

CONTRIBUTORS TO
SEASONAL TIPS AND PHOTOGRAPHY

- **Justin Fox Burks Photography** @justinfoxburks / www.justinfoxburks.com

- **Sarah Symonds** @graceinmyspace / www.graceinmyspace.com

- **Caroline Bivens** @c.b._designs / www.carolinebivensdesigns.com

- **Julie Lancia** @julie.thedesigntwins / www.thedesigntwins.com

- **Jodie Kammerer** @jodie.thedesigntwins / www.thedesigntwins.com

- **Kelly Radcliff** @thetatteredpew / www.thetatteredpew.com

- **Jennifer Ingram** @graciousspaces / www.gracious-spaces.net

- **Jenny Caspers** @acleanprismlife / www.acleanprismlife.com

- **Kathy Atkins** @beautifullyadorned / www.livebeautifullyadorned.com

- **Brandy Bell** @sobellandco / www.sobellandco.com

- **Whitney Herndon** @thegracegraffiti / www.gracegraffiti.com

- **Jenny Scholten** @scholten_family_ceo

- **Pamela Saumure** @pamela.saumure

- **Arianne Miller** @millhousestyle

- Cover photo courtesy of **Kate Riley**. Blog CentSationalstyle.com / Portfolio KateRiley.net

A very special thank you to Stylecraft Home Collection, and Greg and Meredith Drumwright for allowing us to photograph your spaces and furnishings!

ABOUT THE AUTHOR

Victoria Duerstock is a writer, blogger, teacher, and speaker. With a mission to help women seek God's purpose in their lives and with more than twenty years' experience in the furniture and home-design industry, she uses her creativity to inspire hope in readers and ignite bigger dreams. She writes for the blogs Encouraging Women Today, Everything's Gravy, and Creative Corner, and has contributed to multiple devotionals.

Victoria enjoys an active speaking ministry to women and a teaching schedule where she shares essential elements to building an author platform through social media. Read more at VictoriaDuerstock.com.